LEARNING TO SKI

Edited by
Duncan Prowse

Contributors and consultants
David Vine, presenter of BBC Television's *Ski Sunday* programme.
Alan Hole, Staff Coach, English Ski Council.
John Shedden, Director of Coaching, English Ski Council.
Maurice Willoughby, Ski Correspondent of the *Daily Mail*, London,
BASI instructor, member of the 1948 British Olympic Ski Team.
Greg Levitt, Headmaster, Vice-Chairman of
the English Schools Ski Association.
Dennis Nelson, physical education instructor, BASI Coach.
Paddy Smith, Schools Abroad Ski Executive.
Gail Brownrigg, Austrian Ski School instructor.

Illustrations by
Gerard Pestarque

Designed by
Valerie Sargent

Cartoons by
David Lock

Project Development Manager for Schools Abroad
Barbara Hopper

Chancerel

ISBN 0-905703-60-X

© Chancerel Publishers/Schools Abroad 1981
© Chancerel Publishers 1979

All rights reserved. No part of this publication may be reproduced, recorded, transmitted or stored in any retrieval system, in any form whatsoever, without the written permission of the copyright holders.

Chancerel Publishers Ltd.,
40 Tavistock Street,
London WC2E 7PB.

Schools Abroad Group,
Grosvenor Hall,
Bolnore Road,
Haywards Heath,
West Sussex RH16 4BX.

Produced by Chancerel Publishers Ltd.
Graphic reproduction by ReproSharp Ltd., London
and La Cromolito, Milan.
Printed by Fakenham Press Ltd., Norfolk, England.

Photographs

Allsport	6, 7, 8, 9, 10, 13, 14, 44, 54, 64, 72, 73, 83
Ardblair Sports	4(2), 5, 6, 85
Jean Bell	15
Colorsport	Cover, 9, 10, 11, 12
Alan Hole	52, 62, 63, 74
John Noble	76, 78, 79
Mervyn Rees	16, 22, 23, 26, 28(2), 30(3), 32, 33, 37, 42, 45, 46, 48, 50, 53, 56
John Ellis Roberts	16, 29, 79
John Shedden	12, 15(2), 24, 25(2), 26, 39, 47, 60, 63, 68, 69, 71, 75
Ski Club of GB	80(4), 81(2), 82(2), 84, 87
Swiss Federal Avalanche Service	29
Swiss National Tourist Office	31(3), 36, 87(2)
Tony Stone	69
Swedish Tourist Office	76
Maurice Willoughby	81, 83, 84(5), 85(2)

Contents

Introduction by Ingemar Stenmark 4
  The silent superstar; Stenmark's career milestones 5

Chapter I
The World Cup — the white circus 6
  World Cup events 6
The Winter Olympics 8
  Events of the Olympic Games 9
Cross country and ski jumping 10
  Jumping and flying 11
Freestyle skiing 12
  The World Speed Record 13
Skiing for Britain 14
  Young stars to watch; Starting competitive skiing 15

Chapter II
Choosing a resort 16
  Reading a piste map 17
Keeping fit between ski seasons 18
  Daily fitness programme;
  Further pointers to fitness; 19
  The step test 19
Training for skiing 20
  Strength and stamina circuit; Suppleness circuit; 20
  Using weights for training 21
Ski clothing 22
  Ski clothing checklist 23
Boots, skis, bindings and sticks 24
  Ski bindings; Skis; Ski sticks 25
Weather and the skier 26
  Snow and the skier 27
Safety on the slopes 28
  If there should be an accident; The Skiway Code 29
Taking the skilift 30
  If you fall off the drag lift 31

Chapter III
Collecting your equipment 32
  Off to ski school 33
Putting on skis 34
  Stepping into your bindings; The right length
  for ski sticks 35
Coping with skis 36
  Becoming accustomed to your skis 36
On the move 38
  Turning on the level — the clock turn 38
  Turning on the level — the star turn 39
Stepping up the slope 40
  Sidestepping uphill; The herringbone step 41
The first run 42
  Schussing; Developing your balance 43

Falling down and getting up again 44
  Getting up after a fall; Putting on skis on a slope 45
Learning to snowplough 46
  Snowplough — the stance; Gliding and braking 47
Time to turn 48
  Freedom at last; Linking up your turns 49
Traversing and sideslipping 50
  Traversing exercises; Sideslipping 51
Skid into parallels 52
  The plough swing; Where to practise 53
Working towards parallels 54
  Basic swing turns; Pole planting 55
Better parallel turns 56
  Reducing the skid; Increase your angulation 57
Other ways to ski parallel 58
  The direct method; The fan method 59
Compression turns 60
  Compression basic swings; Compression parallels 61
Coping with moguls 62
  Choosing a line; Where do bumps come from? 63
Advanced techniques 64
  Short swings 65
Reading the mountainside 66
  Where to ski 67
Powder snow and ice 68
  Skiing on ice 69
Techniques for racing 70
  The step turn; The skating turn 71
Slalom, Giant Slalom and Downhill 72
  Downhill racing 73
Artificial ski slopes 74
  Find your nearest ski slope; Ski Tests 75

Chapter IV
Ski touring away from it all 76
Skiing to the top of the world 78
  Conquering the Haute Route 79

Chapter V
Norse hunters and mad British 80
The new international sport 82
New equipment, new techniques 84
Ski history charted 86

Chapter VI
French for skiers 88
German for skiers 90
Italian for skiers 92
Glossary 94
Index 95
You and your group 96

Introduction by Ingemar Stenmark

Skiing is a wonderful and exciting sport. This book is an interesting and useful guide for young skiers and from it you can gain a wealth of information about where to go, what to do and how to ski.

I hope that each of you enjoys skiing and being in the mountains as much as I have. Good skiing!

Ingemar Stenmark

Below: *Stenmark at the 1980 Olympics.*　　**Above:** *Stenmark with World Cup medals.*

The silent superstar

A favourite past-time of sports fans is comparing champions of the past with the current stars. But as far as skiing is concerned, there is no contest. Ingemar Stenmark of Sweden is the greatest skier there has ever been.

He paces a race even better than runners like Sebastian Coe and Steve Ovett. His technical ability is obvious, even to someone watching the slalom for the first time. He can leave himself so far behind on the clock after the first run, that his chances look hopeless.

Then comes the famous Stenmark charge. It's enough to put a commentator out of work. The way he weaves his way through the maze of slalom gates, down a slope you can't even walk on, defies description.

Stenmark himself is rarely prepared to describe it either. He is a man of very few words. You are lucky to get a terse comment: "It was good for me today."

More often than not, the quiet and lonely man of the slopes will ask you to excuse him, and walk slowly away from an interview and from the crowds who have just cheered and marvelled at his latest performance.

Yet inspite of his hate of publicity, his fans are faithful. In a recent popularity poll run by a Swedish newspaper, the result was, 1: Ingemar Stenmark; 2: Bjorn Borg; 3: His majesty the King of Sweden.

David Vine

Stenmark's career milestones

By the end of the 1981 ski season, Ingemar Stenmark had won more World Cup races than any other skier, male or female, before him. His total now stands at 62 victories.

Anne-Marie Moser Proell of Austria also has 62 wins to her name, but some of these are combined points results, not actual race victories.

Since he first began to dominate World Cup slalom racing in 1976, at the age of 20, Stenmark has taken the overall World Cup title three times, in 1976, 1977, 1978. In 1979 the rules under which World Cup points are distributed were changed. Whether this was the intention of the authorities or not, the new system has worked against Stenmark, as he regularly wins the slalom and giant slalom races but seldom even competes in the downhill. Even so, he is not far behind — in overall points he was second to Phil Maher of America in the 1981 World Cup.

Since 1976 he has won the slalom seven times and the giant slalom six times.

Ingemar Stenmark was born at Tarneby in Sweden on March 18, 1956. Encouraged by his father, he began racing young. In his first year at school he won his first victory.

After he left school he took up full time ski racing and, trained by the Swedish coach Olle Roller, he was soon a member of the Swedish A Ski Team. In his first international senior competition, he won the prestigious Kandahar Cup.

Stenmark's method of training is unusual but obviously effective. It consists of cycling, long distance running and, in order to develop his balance, tight rope walking and riding a unicycle.

Although other ski stars are now chipping away at Stenmark's premier position in the sport, he is still among the top World Cup competitors. He will also, no doubt, play a major part in the 1982 World Championships at Schladming, Austria.

However, he will not be able to take part in the 1984 Winter Olympics at Sarajevo, Yugoslavia, as he is no longer technically an amateur.

Above: *A monocycle for balance training. Stenmark's training schedule also includes long distance running, cycling and even tight rope walking.*

Although Stenmark did not win any medals at the 1976 Games, early in his career of international stardom, he did take the Gold medals for both the slalom and giant slalom at the 1980 Winter Games, at Lake Placid.

Since then he has taken out a B Licence, which allows him (and other skiers) a degree of professional status.

I. The World Cup – the white circus

If you are lucky enough to be on the slopes at a World Cup race, you will almost certainly catch sight of a giant of a man, in a specially made black ski suit, trudging his way through the snow, leaving imprints like pot holes. His name is Serge Lang, a journalist, and he is the man who was responsible for the formation of the world's most important ski competition, the World Cup.

For the first year he ran the competition unofficially, but in 1967 he and his colleagues obtained the support of skiing's international governing body, the FIS (the International Ski Federation). As a result that winter produced the first official races and the first men's and women's champions. They were Jean Claude Killy of France, who won almost everything, and Nancy Greene of Canada.

Today the World Cup dominates the sport in the mountains of Europe, Japan and North America. It has become known as the White Circus, involving hundreds of ski racers and many more in back-up teams and race organisation, plus an army of television, radio and press followers. It's *The* Snow Show.

The three disciplines

World Cup racing consists of three different disciplines – **downhill, slalom** and **giant slalom**. Each has become very specialised. Although some racers take part in all three events, the principal interest is in the downhill. Its speed and danger make it the blue riband of skiing.

The battle for the men's downhill of 1981 was fought

Below: *Alexander Zhirov, the Soviet Union's new ski star.*

Above: *Stenmark with some of his 60 World Cup trophies.*

out over ten races in Germany, France, Switzerland, Austria and the United States. The races were held on some of the toughest courses in World Cup history.

The racers had to push themselves to their limits and beyond, which resulted in a series of terrifying falls. With the time clock ticking away and each competitor knowing that over the three mile course, hundredths of a second would make all the difference, they went faster and faster – up to 135kph (85mph) and more.

Ken Read of Canada crashed at Garmisch. Uli Spiess of Austria started the season with a triumph at Val Gardena in Italy. He was the only racer to take the infamous triple bump, the Camel's Humps, by jumping off the first and clearing the others in one. One other competitor had tried in practice and ended up in hospital. Spiess dared and won the race. Ironically he smashed a leg later in training in Saint Moritz, and was out for the season.

The season as a whole will probably be best remembered for the crash of the Downhill Championship leader, Peter Müller. On the longest and most famous hill of all, the Lamberhorn at Wengen, Müller came out of the final two S bends, with only 25 metres to go, *in the air*. He lost control, crashed through the straw bales and into the crowd at 130kph (82mph). Crowd and commentators alike thought that he was dead. But he sustained nothing more than a fractured shoulder and he was skiing again in four weeks.

At the end of it all Harti Weirather of Austria just pipped Canada's Steve Podborski to the trophy.

In what are called the technical disciplines, slalom and giant slalom, Ingemar Stenmark of Sweden is still the man everyone wants to beat. After more than 60 victories, he has still retained his amazingly high standards and his will to win. But the signs are that Stenmark is finding the pace harder and harder to maintain.

The Mahre brothers, Phil and Steve from the United States, and the Soviet Union's new star, Alexander Zhirov, are bidding for his titles.

Future stars to watch

The prospects for the new season, this year as every year, will have all those who follow the sport sitting on the edges of their seats — whether it is an armchair in front of the fire and the television, or a hard chair in a cold commentary box by the finishing line.

For the last few years Anne Marie Moser Pröell of Austria has dominated the women's events. But with her retirement the girls have been having an exciting tussle for supremacy. Erika Hess of Switzerland, Tamara McKinney of America, Cornelia Pröell of Austria (Anne Marie's younger sister) and Torill Fjeldstad of Norway are all racers to watch in the future.

For those who like statistics, this is how one American ski magazine described the whole season of men's World Cup racing: 'The 30,000 mile ski race, which went through 31 events, 20 ski areas and eight different countries on three continents'.

Figures give some idea of the scope of the White Circus, but in words it is enough to say that it is the ultimate test of skill, determination, endurance, courage and perfection of technique yet devised for ski racers.

Below: *Moser Pröell has dominated women's skiing.*

Events of the World Cup
Downhill

Downhill courses vary between 3.25 and 4km (2-2.5 miles). The men's courses have a vertical fall of up to 1,000 metres (3,250ft) and the women's 700 metres (2,300ft). The courses are designed to test a skier's skill and stamina with fast straight runs, bumps, dips and turns between steep and icy descents.

Slalom (special slalom)

Sometimes called special slalom. The competitor has to follow a route between poles (called **gates**) set 4-5 metres (13-16.5ft) apart. The men's course is betwen 400 and 600 metres long (440-600 yards) with between 55 and 75 gates (average 60). Some gates are set horizontally with poles side by side across the slope (open gates), some are set vertically, with poles one above the other (closed gates) and some set at an angle (oblique gates). The women's course is run over the same distance, but with 45-60 (average 50) gates only. Slalom is a test of a skier's control and turning technique.

Giant slalom

Giant slalom is similar to special slalom, but on a larger scale, being over a greater distance (the course is 1,500 metres, approximately one mile, long) and with a greater vertical fall 250-400m (825-1,300ft). Competitors ski faster than in special slalom. The gates are twin poles with a square banner between them, set 4-8 metres (13-26ft) apart.

The Winter Olympics

In spite of all the other, headline-catching competitions in the world of skiing, the Olympic Games still has a special place in the career of any racer. That career is bound to be short and the Olympics only happen every four years, so few skiers manage more than one chance to win the cherished gold medal.

In the World Cup, which is a whole season of tests of ability and performance, there is always the next race, or even the next season. In the Games there is no second bite at the cherry. Suddenly one morning, when conditions are probably quite unlike those under which most training and preparation took place, the racer is at the starting gate with just one chance.

One mistake and it's all over; one brilliant performance and it's medals on the podium. Either way the competitors will all remember it for the rest of their lives.

All those who have reached the Olympics say that nothing matches the pressure and tension in the Olympic Village. It builds up gradually until the moment before the competitor skis off from the top of the hill.

One man who not only survived that pressure, but emerged to produce the Olympic performance that is still most talked about and most often repeated on television, was Franz Klammer of Austria.

The hero of '76

The 1976 Winter Olympics were held at Innsbruck, not too far from Klammer's home village. The defending champion was Bernard Russi of Switzerland, the glamorous star of the sport who had set an excellent time on the demanding and spectacular Patcherkofel course. Klammer was drawn number 15, the last of the top group. He exploded out of the gate. He had a season of wins behind him, but this was the one he wanted most of all.

Austrian fans, and a worldwide television audience, held their breaths, as he looked to be out of control — arms and legs everywhere. Surely he had to crash any second? There was almost complete silence in the crowd, until the moment that he whipped past the electronic timing device at the finish.

Below: *Ingemar Stenmark (Sweden), winner of two gold medals at the 1980 Winter Olympics at Lake Placid.*

Above: *Franz Klammer (Austria) Downhill gold, 1976.*

A golden smile

Ingemar Stenmark of Sweden had to wait until the 1980 Games at Lake Placid in the United States to score gold. But by then he had been at the top long enough for some experts to believe that he would not be able to withstand the unique pressure of the Olympics.

He more than withstood it, he won twice. He took the gold medals in both the giant slalom and the slalom. After the second race, when he realised that he had won, he actually smiled. And the Stenmark smile made bigger headlines than his double gold!

The next Olympics are not until 1984, when they will be held in and around the Yugoslavian town of Sarajevo. This will be the first time that the Winter Olympics have been held in Eastern Europe. The resort of Jahorina will stage the women's events, while the men's events will be held in Bjelasnica.

The medallists of 1984 are probably already competing on some or all of the competitive ski circuits. But because of the rules banning professionals some famous names will not be there. The only full professionals in the world of skiing are a small group of Americans and past European champions, who make up the Pro-ski Circus, in the United States. They are unable to take part in either the World Cup or the Olympics.

The semi-professionals, like Stenmark, who hold what are called B Licences can compete in the World Cup and World Championships, but not the Olympics. All other competitors are officially amateurs. This means that they are supported by grants from their national ski federations, which in turn very often have sponsorship links with manufacturers of ski equipment.

Events of the Winter Olympics

The Winter Olympics have had a stormy history, with much opposition from those who believe that skiing is too commercial a sport to be included in the amateur Olympic programme. The first Games in 1924 at Chamonix were only given Olympic status two years after they were held. Here is a list of present day events:

Nordic events

Biathlon (20km, 12.5 mile, cross country with four target shots); Biathlon Relay (4 × 7.5km, 4.5 miles, with two shots); Men's 15km Cross Country; Men's 30km Cross Country; Men's 50km Cross Country; Men's 4 × 10km Relay; 70 metre Ski Jump; 90 metre Ski Jump; Nordic Combined (15km, 9.3 miles, cross country with jumping); Women's 5km Cross Country; Women's 10km Cross Country; Women's 3 × 5km Relay.

Alpine events

Men's Downhill; Men's Giant Slalom; Men's Slalom; Women's Downhill, Women's Giant Slalom; Women's Slalom.

Skating

Men's Figure Skating; Men's 500 metres Speed Skating; Men's 1,500 metres Speed Skating; Men's 5,000 metres Speed Skating; Men's 10,000 metres Speed Skating; Women's Figure Skating; Women's 500 metres Speed Skating; Women's 1,000 metres Speed Skating; Women's 1,500 metres Speed Skating; Women's 3,000 metres Speed Skating; Pairs Figure Skating.

Other events

Two-man Bobsleigh; Four-man Bobsleigh; Ice Hockey; Men's Single Seater Luge; Men's Two Seater Luge; Women's Single Seater Luge.

Above: *Schladming, Austria, 1982 venue.*

The World Championships

Skiing's other major contest, apart from the World Cup and the Olympic Games, is the World Championship, held under the auspices of the FIS. This takes place every four years, alternating with the Olympics. The event lasts 12 days. The next World Championships are to be held at Schladming in Austria in 1982. In the past this little resort has had weather problems, so the organisers are hoping for better than usual conditions.

Cross country and ski jumping

Nordic skiing was once the only form of the sport. But in recent times it has been completely overshadowed by the excitement of the Alpine slalom and downhill races. But now the Nordic events are being more and more hotly contested every year, with the Russians and the East Germans leading the field, especially in the Olympic Games.

In the 1980 Winter Games at Lake Placid, in America, only one non-jumping event was *not* won by a Russian or an East German. Thomas Wassberg of Sweden managed to take the Men's 15km Cross Country gold and thus prevent an Eastern bloc clean sweep. Britain's Keith Oliver has had some excellent performances, with a 16th

Every year Nordic World Cups are held for both jumping and cross country. The Scandinavians and the Austrians are still dominant in the jumping. All the results from a season of cross country racing and jumping are put together to produce an overall winner. The 1981 Men's Jumping Champion was Armin Kogler of Austria. Alexandre Zavjalov (USSR) won the Men's Cross Country and Reiser Smetanina (USSR) won the Women's Cross Country. There is no recognised women's ski jumping competition.

Below left: *Target shooting in the Olympic Biathlon.*
Below: *Olympic Men's Cross Country.*

place at Lake Placid in 1980, and an 11th place at Sapporo, Japan, in 1972.

Cross country races at all international levels are held over undulating courses designed to test the endurance of competitors to the maximum. For men, a 15km race is considered a sprint and 50km is a marathon. Women race over shorter distances — sprinting on courses 5km and 10km long.

The Vasa race in Sweden is even longer at 85.5km (53.5 miles). It is so popular now that the entry is limited to 10,000 people each year. Even more people take part in the Engadine Marathon in Switzerland every March. In 1981 there were 11,695 participants, of which 38 men and seven ladies came from Britain. The Engadine course covers 42km (26 miles).

In the Olympics and most Nordic races, apart from the mass marathons, competitors start off at regular intervals and are timed over the distance of the course. Some events are team relays with four men or women, each covering a certain distance.

Biathlon is the military cousin of cross country racing. Competitors ski to certain points where they shoot at targets. It doesn't take much imagination to realise that after skiing several kilometres, arms and legs turn to jelly and holding a rifle steady is extremely difficult.

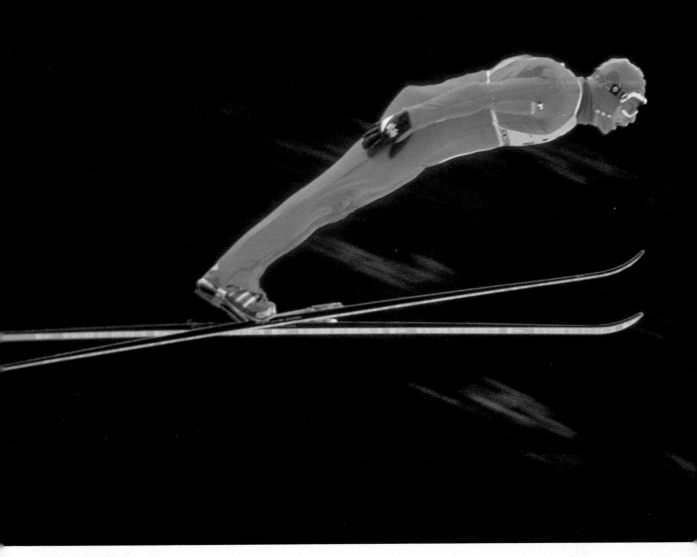

Jumping and Flying

Ski jumping is perhaps the most spectacular of all the skiing events and it is the shop window, the television eye-catcher of Nordic skiing. In the Olympics and the World Cup there are two different types — the 70 metre jump and the 90 metre jump. Confusingly, this does not refer to the actual height of the hill, but to a complex combination of measurements.

The high spot of the ski jumping season is the famous Four Hills Tournament, over Christmas and New Year. There are jumps at Bischofshofen, Garmisch (where the 1936 Olympics took place), Innsbruck (1976 Olympics) and Oberstdorf.

Jumpers are not only aiming to make the longest jump, they are also marked for their style in the air and their landing. So the longest jump does not necessarily win. The unofficial world record distance for a ski jump is 181m (593ft), by Bogdan Norcic of Yugoslavia, but he fell on landing so his distance does not count. Armin Kogler of Austria holds the official world record, with a jump of 180m (590ft) at the ski flying hill at Oberstdorf in February 1981.

To give you an idea of what it is like to jump this distance, imagine someone taking off from the top of

Above: *Karl Schnabl (Austria) Olympic gold, 1976.*

Saint Paul's Cathedral and flying the length of Wembley Stadium, all at 110kph (70mph)! While doing this the jumper has to concentrate on the position of his arms, keeping his skis together and remaining in control, as these are also points the judges watch for.

Karl Schnabl of Austria, who won a ski jumping gold medal at the Bergisel Hill in Innsbruck at the 1976 Olympics, has described setting off from the top of the hill as, "jumping off the end of one world, hoping there is another nearby to land on." In the case of the Bergisel, this is particularly apt, as from the take off point the jumper has a superb view of the Innsbruck cemetary!

For the world's best ski jumpers even the Olympic and World Cup events are not enough. There is even a ski flying contest, which takes place on the largest jumping hills of all. Because of the extreme height of the hill and the speed the jumpers attain, they actually fly for a short period — aerodynamically supported on a cushion of air below their skis.

Until recently this event was judged only on distance. But now style points have been introduced to the competition, making it very similar to ordinary jumping, only faster and higher.

Freestyle skiing

The 1960s were years of innovation in many things, from pop music to women's rights. In the late 1960s skiing too developed its own liberation movement, which began as the sport of hot dogging and became what is now called freestyle.

All over the world, ski schools have been quick to adopt the winning techniques of champion skiers and make them into text book examples. Typically, it was in the United States that skiers began to throw away the rule books and ski with wild and exuberant circus tricks over rough mogul fields. Until then moguls, which are caused by many skiers carving out hollows as they turn, had been considered nothing but a nuisance.

Soon the jumps, leaps and tricks of hot dogging became popular in many parts of America. The first hot dog contest was held at Aspen in the Rockies in 1971.

Since then many other events have been added to the freestyle repertoire, like ballet, which is a series of graceful movements, sometimes performed in groups and to music. Various stunts have catchy names, like *The Daffy* (legs spread as far as possible, one in front and the other behind) and the *Outrigger* (one ski on edge, held out to one side). Aerials are mid-air tricks, like *Helicopter Spins*. Inversions are somersaults and Uprights like the *Star Jump* are mid-air splits. Some freestylers have even managed triple toe loops (as in skating) and triple back somersaults. Hot dogging has remained the speciality of the mogul bashers.

Freestyle began to attract a major following in Europe in the mid-1970s and the British are now among the top performers. The FIS now officially backs a Freestyle World Cup. In Britain there are even freestyle demonstrations on artificial slopes, like the one set up every year for the Daily Mail Ski Show.

Above: *Hotdog skiing.* **Below:** *Jim Garrison watches Wayne Wong. Both were freestyle pioneers in America.*

Above: *Steve McKinney, on his record-breaking 200kph run at Portillo, Chile, in 1978.*

The World Speed Record

Attempts at the World Speed Record on skis, the fastest average speed over one kilometre, constitute the most dangerous and extraordinary of all the fringe events in the world of skiing.

The *Kilometro Lanciato*, the Flying Kilometre course in Cervinia, Italy, is the usual venue for speed record attempts. It was there in July 1978 that Steve McKinney of the United States set a record of 198kph (123mph) that brought him within a hair's breadth of the magic 200kph mark.

In order to achieve speeds like this skiers must adopt the egg position, making their bodies as streamlined as possible. They wear special aerodynamically designed helmets. The problem is to keep the skis in contact with the snow. If the skier becomes airborne he slows up immediately as well as losing control. If this happens

disaster is never far away. In a world record attempt in 1974, the Swiss skier, Jean Béguelin, ran off the track and was killed.

Following his success at Cervinia, McKinney and several other top speed aces met at a specially prepared course at the resort of Portillo in Chile, South America, in October 1978. McKinney broke the 200kph (124.5mph) barrier by a fraction of a second. Two other skiers, Mark Rowan of Canada and Ben Lindberg of Sweden came within two kilometres an hour of the record. At times on the course all three of them were travelling at almost 210kph (131mph). The toughest part, according to McKinney, is slowing down at the end!

The women too have now entered the field of pure speed. Catherine Breyton of France clocked up the women's world record at Silverton, Colorado, USA, in April 1981. Her official speed was 169.332kph (105.83mph).

Skiing for Britain

With a Polish father, a home in Austria and ski racing for Holland (he has a Dutch passport) no wonder everyone laughed when we said, "He's British!"

His name didn't help either — Konrad Bartelski. But Bartelski was, and is, British despite his name and his parentage. In the years he raced for the Dutch, he always wore a crash helmet with a Union Jack proudly painted on the side and was waiting for the chance to get back into the British team after a misunderstanding, as it was officially called, had forced him out of it.

Eventually he was welcomed back in time for the Olympic Games of 1980 at Lake Placid, USA. This time, with his other passport, a British one, Konrad Bartelski (GBR) put up Britain's best ever Olympic performance by a male racer. He finished 12th in the Downhill, the blue riband of the sport, and was only three seconds (go on, count them to see how little time that it is . . .) slower than the champion and gold medallist. And that was on a course 3,000 metres long, taken at 130kph (80mph) down the frozen side of Whiteface mountain.

Until that moment, lunchtime on February 14th 1980, Britian's finest moments were as far back as the 1968 Games in Grenoble, France, when Jeremy Palmer-Tomkinson finished 25th in the Downhill.

The girls had done better — Gina Hathorn missed a bronze medal in the slalom by a fraction in 1968 and then, four years later in Japan, Davina Galica came seventh in the giant slalom. However, Bartelski's 12th in the number one race, the Men's Downhill, overshadows even those excellent performances.

No excuses are needed for using the word excellent when talking about fourth, seventh, and 12th places. But what about a British third, second, or even first?

Since the war, skiing has developed enormously in Britain both on snow and on plastic slopes. It's no longer a sport just for the rich and the privileged, which is where we went wrong in the past.

Nowadays, places like Cairngorm, Glenshee and Glencoe in Scotland are packed with thousands of holidaymakers on skis and top international racers are being attracted to the British championship races held there on the snow covered Scottish heather.

Our downhill championship race is usually held in Val d'Isère in France and although we lack the really big mountains, the ever increasing number of plastic slopes provide the chance for many people, and especially youngsters, to get on the boards just down the road, before going abroad for the real thing.

It is this growth in the sport in Britain — a growth helped in no small way by the exposure skiing now gets on television — that is raising the standards of our international racers. The organisation of our teams abroad is also improving and in the past there has been plenty of room for that.

This season, it will not be Konrad Bartelski, the one man show. One young racer in particular is already making us all sit up and take notice. Don't expect him to beat the world — at least not this season — but watch out for a 17-year-old flying out of Scotland. His name is Martin Bell.

Below: *Konrad Bartelski, Britain's top skier.*

Young stars to watch

Martin Bell Born in Cheshire, lives in Edinburgh. Martin is one of the best British skiers for a long time. He is now ranked fifth in the world for his age. He had an extremely successful racing season in Australia and New Zealand, during the southern hemisphere winter of 1981, competing against senior World Cup stars. During the northern winter Martin attends the famous ski school at Stamms, in Austria, where normal lessons are combined with intensive ski training.

Sarah Lewis From Sandown Park Ski Racing Club, one of Britain's top junior artificial slope racers. She is in the England and British Junior Squads and won one of the two Schools Abroad Young Skier of the Year Awards in 1981.

Tania Adams From Bearsden Ski Club in Scotland, Tania has recently had to make the agonising decision whether to take the offer of a place in the Scottish Ballet or to ski with the Scottish Junior Squad. She chose skiing.

Graham Bell Younger brother of Martin and showing great promise.

Lesley Beck From Dunbarton, she shows outstanding talent in the slalom. Even though she is a junior she has reached the British Senior Team.

Nigel Smith, from Sandown Park and **Nick Fellows**, the other Schools Abroad Young Skier of the Year 1981, are other young British skiers with good prospects.

Above: *Martin Bell at 17 is Britain's top junior skier and is now ranked fifth in the world for his age.*
Left: *Sara Lewis, a member of the British Junior ski team.*
Right: *Nick Fellows, with Sara Lewis, joint winner of the 1981 Schools Abroad Young Skier of the Year Award.*

Starting competitive skiing

If you want to ski competitively, the first thing to do is find your nearest ski club. There are clubs all over Britain now, many of them with their own artificial ski slopes.

Representatives of the ski clubs make up the **Ski Councils** of each of the Home Nations — England, Scotland, Wales and Northern Ireland. These Councils are responsible for promoting skiing in their own countries and are supported by the Sports Council. Representatives of each Ski Council make up the **British Ski Federation**, which is responsible for British competitions and British international teams.

To find out where your nearest ski club is, write to your national Ski Council. They can also provide you with information about artificial slopes and competitions in your area (see page 75).

Club racing results are automatically forwarded to the Regional Ski Associations and Ski Councils, so if you are winning club races, you will soon be asked to take the next step up the ladder. The Ski Council coaches keep in constant touch with club instructors.

The next step is to take part in the selection races held regionally to choose the **Regional Junior Squads**. Most junior competitions are held in age groups of 12-13, 14-15 and 16-18.

If you are winning races at Regional and National Junior levels you will be invited to take part in selection for your National Junior Squad. As a member of the National Junior Squads, or if you are good enough, the British Junior Squad, you will have the chance to take part in training programmes, very often in the Alps.

II. Choosing a resort

Resorts have come a long way since the early days of skiing, half a century ago. Then, roads were often blocked in winter and only resorts on the railway, like Chamonix, could be reached easily.

Once in the resort, skiers usually had to walk up the mountain, carrying their equipment, before they could ski down again. Certain places in Switzerland were better organised. You posted your skis at the bottom of the hill and the postman walked up beside you, carrying them!

Today skiing is the favourite sport of millions of people and communications have changed accordingly. Aircraft and buses bring people to the resorts. And once there, they have everything from cable cars (developed from the winding gear of mine cages) to drag lifts to make sure that they can spend as much time as possible actually skiing.

Which resort?

There are many different factors to consider in deciding where to ski. **Which country** to go to is one of the first things to decide. Most people choose the Alps, which means France, Switzerland, Austria or Italy. But there are good and inexpensive ski resorts in Yugoslavia and Bulgaria. Many people from Europe now ski in the United States and facilities in Scotland have improved greatly. When deciding which country to visit, here are some points to consider:

★ **The distance you will have to travel** (bus or air?).
★ **The exchange rate and the cost of incidentals.**
★ **Whether or not you speak the language** (is this important to you?).

Below: *Traditional chalets, Morgins.*

Below: *New apartments, Avoriaz.*

The next thing to think about is what **kind of resort** might suit you. These are some of the choices:
★ **An old village with character** (not necessarily well planned for skiers).
★ **A purpose-built resort** (often with apartment accommodation).
★ **A small ski station** (isolated, but good value).

It is important to consider early on when you wish to go, for there is a great deal of difference in cost between **high** and **low seasons**. If your party can travel in the term time, rather than the peak periods of Christmas, half-term and Easter, your skiing will be more economical.

By now you will probably have selected several places. Here are some more points by which to compare them.
★ **The transfer time from the airport to the resort.**
★ **The range of skiing available** (the altitude difference between the top ski station and the village, and thus the length of the ski runs).
★ **The snow record and length of the season.**

Lifts and ski runs

Probably the most important thing of all is the **ski lift** and **ski run** system in the resort. In many resorts lifts are owned by private companies, although they may also be owned by community cooperatives, or local property owners. Separate ownership can be a problem, since a lift pass may not cover all the lifts in the resort.

How **lift passes** are organised and paid for can vary, too. Beginners sometimes find it best to pay for single trips. This is not usually done with money, but with a **points card**, which is clipped (each run costs a certain number of points) by the ski lift attendant. This, however, can be expensive and inconvenient for the experienced skier.

A lift pass, for one day, or for a six or 13-day period, is the most common way to pay for uphill transport. This also has the advantage that the tour operator organising your holdiay can usually negotiate a special price with the resort authorities.

For most lift passes a **photograph** is necessary. It saves time to take one with you. Some resorts now have special ticket machines that bleep if the pass is valid, and even open the turnstile automatically.

Hotels, meals and après ski

The quality and type of accommodation available varies from country to country and resort to resort. Having chosen either hotel or apartments (according to the resort), it is worth considering whether you prefer accommodation near the slopes or the village (some hotels are near both).

As far as **meals** are concerned, most people return to their hotel for lunch. But keen skiers can usually take packed lunches with them, as long as they order them in advance.

Most resorts today provide a variety of activities for those who want to take a day off skiing, or who are still feeling energetic in the evening (*après ski* means after skiing in French). There may be swimming pools, ice rinks for skating and curling (bowls on ice), tobogganing, plus folk evenings, fondues and, of course discos.

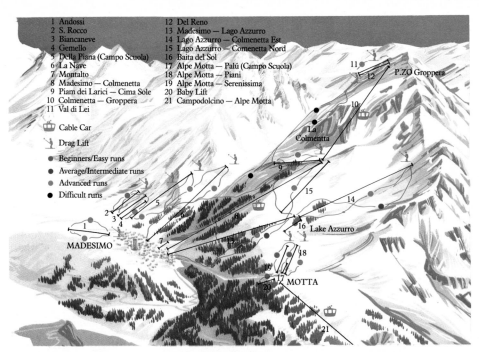

1 Andossi	12 Del Reno
2 S. Rocco	13 Madesimo — Lago Azzurro
3 Biancaneve	14 Lago Azzurro — Colmenetta Est
4 Gemello	15 Lago Azzurro — Comenetta Nord
5 Della Piana (Campo Scuola)	16 Baita del Sol
6 La Nave	17 Alpe Motta — Palú (Campo Scuola)
7 Montalto	18 Alpe Motta — Piani
8 Madesimo — Colmenetta	19 Alpe Motta — Serenissima
9 Piam dei Larici — Cima Sole	20 Baby Lift
10 Colmenetta — Groppera	21 Campodolcino — Alpe Motta
11 Val di Lei	

🚡 Cable Car

⛷ Drag Lift

● Beginners/Easy runs

● Average/Intermediate runs

● Advanced runs

● Difficult runs

MADESIMO

P.ZO Groppera

La Colmentta

Lake Azzurro

MOTTA

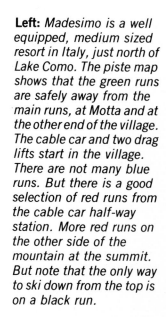

Left: *Madesimo is a well equipped, medium sized resort in Italy, just north of Lake Como. The piste map shows that the green runs are safely away from the main runs, at Motta and at the other end of the village. The cable car and two drag lifts start in the village. There are not many blue runs. But there is a good selection of red runs from the cable car half-way station. More red runs on the other side of the mountain at the summit. But note that the only way to ski down from the top is on a black run.*

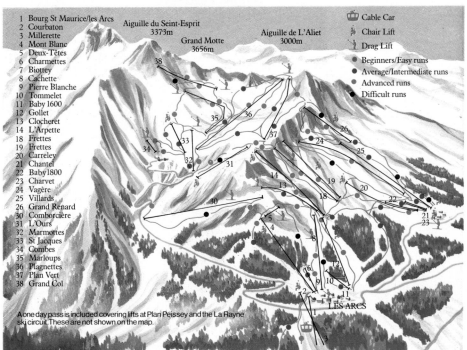

1 Bourg St Maurice/les Arcs	
2 Courbaton	
3 Millerette	
4 Mont Blanc	
5 Deux-Têtes	
6 Charmettes	
7 Biottey	
8 Cachette	
9 Pierre Blanche	
10 Tommelet	
11 Baby 1600	
12 Gollet	
13 Clocheret	
14 L'Arpette	
18 Frettes	
19 Frettes	
20 Carreley	
21 Chantel	
22 Baby1800	
23 Charvet	
24 Vagère	
25 Villards	
26 Grand Renard	
30 Comborcière	
31 L'Ours	
32 Marmottes	
33 St Jacques	
34 Combes	
35 Marloups	
36 Plagnettes	
37 Plan Vert	
38 Grand Col	

Aiguille du Seint-Esprit
3373m

Grand Motte
3656m

Aiguille de L'Aliet
3000m

🚡 Cable Car

🚡 Chair Lift

⛷ Drag Lift

● Beginners/Easy runs

● Average/Intermediate runs

● Advanced runs

● Difficult runs

LES ARCS

A one day pass is included covering lifts at Plan Peissey and the La Rayne ski circuit. These are not shown on the map.

Left: *The modern French resort of Les Arcs has an immense lift system — 38 lifts listed on the piste map. Skiing is on both sides of a ridge, so that there is a range of skiing conditions always available. From the map it is easy to see that it is an excellent resort for intermediate to good skiers. There are green runs for beginners, but not actually in the village. But there are blue runs throughout the network of pistes, so even quite inexperienced skiers can enjoy long and varied runs. A wide choice of red runs is offered plus rather more black runs than usual.*

Reading the piste map

It is essential to be able to read a piste map, both when choosing which resort to visit and when making your way round the resort and slopes. A piste map should tell you:

★ **The type of runs available.** European ski runs are colour coded according to standard. **Green = Beginners; Blue = Intermediate; Red = Good intermediate; Black = Advanced.** Choose a resort with runs to suit the standard of your party. A resort with many green and blue runs will suit a group of beginners. Green and blue runs may be in the village, or as at the Swiss resort of Leysin, high up the mountain, as well. This means intermediate skiers can enjoy the longer runs.

★ **The layout and location of lifts and pistes.** A good system provides a choice of lifts out of the village, so there are no bottlenecks at crowded times of day. It also provides as many linking runs as possible. See which way slopes face — south for sunny skiing; north for longer lasting snow.

★ **The number and type of lifts available.** Each lift usually has a name and the map should show if it is a drag or chair lift, or a cable car.

★ **Some piste maps show the length of the season and the range of skiing available.** These may be available from the resort office. It is advisable to carry a piste map with you when skiing.

Keeping fit between ski seasons

Skiers need to be extra-fit, as skiing requires one of the highest rates of energy expenditure of any sport. But because skiing is so enjoyable and fulfilling, many recreational skiers misjudge their own physical fitness and strength. Some push themselves too hard on the ski slopes. Then, too late, they realise that they were not fit enough to cope with the strain. Sometimes this only happens after a bad fall.

Skiers who are not properly prepared are more likely to injure themselves. You need to strengthen your muscles to protect your joints and bones.

Before you start to train specially for skiing, you must achieve a fair measure of general, all-round fitness.

The first step in fitness training is to build up the efficiency of your heart, lungs and blood flow, so that your muscles can be provided with the energy they need.

To produce energy, your muscles need fuel — oxygen and glucose (sugar). As the work load on your muscles increases, more fuel is needed to power them. In order to provide the extra fuel, your heart beats faster, you breathe faster and deeper and you get hotter. The fitter you are, the less this process will hurt and the more quickly you will recover.

To build up and maintain a reasonable level of all-round fitness, you need to take regular exercise. The best way to do this is to follow a **daily fitness programme**. This should contain a balanced set of exercises, designed to tone up your whole body and improve the efficiency of your heart and lungs.

Try to exercise at the same time each day — not straight after meals. Make sure you have time to complete all three groups in the chart below.

Daily fitness programme

Group 1 — choose one or the other

Jogging	1-2 miles	Immediately after
Cycling	3-5 miles	exercise, feel your pulse. If it is under 120 per minute, you are not working hard enough.

Group 2 — chose any two exercises

Running on the spot	3 mins	Repeat each exercise twice, with a short rest of
Skipping	3 mins	about 2 mins between
Running upstairs, walking down	10 times	each one.
Stride jumping	3 mins	

Group 3 — choose two from each section

a) Feet astride; one arm behind back; rotate other arm; alternate.
b) Feet astride; arms bent; rotate both arms in together.

Concentrate on making each movement as smooth and strong as possible, rather than on speed or number of repetitions. Do each exercise 5-10 times.

a) Crouch; keep hands flat on ground; straighten legs.
b) Bending to right and left.
c) Hands clasped; twist trunk.
d) Punch right with left arm; and left with right arm.
e) Clasp feet, straighten legs.

a) Stand up; bend knees; hands on knees; push up again.
b) Lie on back; raise legs; swing down to floor sideways.
c) Bicycling in the air (50 times).
d) Crouch; jump in air; land feet astride; jump to crouch.

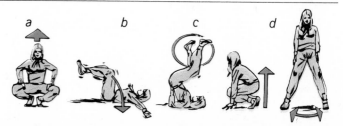

The step test

As early as 1899 it was discovered that top Nordic skiers often had enlarged hearts. Since then it has become well known that an essential part of all training is improving the effectiveness of the heart in pumping blood round the arteries.

It is easy to measure how your heart is performing, by taking your pulse rate — counting the number of heartbeats (or pulses, usually felt in the wrist) every minute. An athlete's heart tends to be larger and therefore able to pump more blood with fewer beats than the heart of an average person. A top international competitor may have a pulse rate as low as 35 per minute. A fit athlete would have a rate of about 60 per minute and the average man's heart rate is about 72 per minute. Women average about 78.

A simple way to test your own fitness is to discover how fast your heart recovers (and your pulse rate slows down) after exercise. The step test is one way of doing this.

★ **Find a sturdy box or low chair,** about 50cm (18ins) high.

★ **Step up onto it and down from it with alternate feet, every two seconds for five minutes;**

★ **Rest for one minute;**

★ **Find the carotid artery in your neck, and count your pulse rate for 30 seconds.** Rest for 30 seconds. Count a second time. Rest again. Count a third time. Now calculate your results.

Above: *Step ups are good exercises for skiers. You can also use a small step (a bathroom stool, or anything strong that is about 50cm (18ins) high) to test your level of fitness. Follow the instructions above.*

Calculate your results

a) Add up your three pulse counts:

Count 1 = 70
Count 2 = 66
Count 3 = 59
Total = **195**

b) Double your total: 2 × 195 = **390**

c) Multiply the number of seconds you spent performing the exercise (5 minutes = 300 seconds) by 100:   300 × 100 = **30,000**

d) Divide c) by b):   30,000 ÷ 390 = **74.3**

e) Now read off your total on the graph below:

Step test result chart

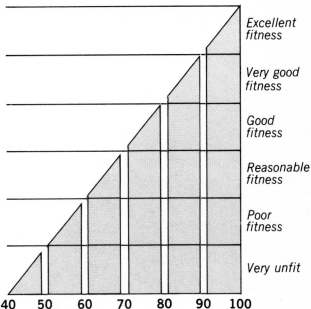

Excellent fitness

Very good fitness

Good fitness

Reasonable fitness

Poor fitness

Very unfit

40 50 60 70 80 90 100

Further pointers to fitness

★ **Take every opportunity to exercise** — try swimming, country walking, yoga, gymnastics, roller skating, dancing.

★ **Try some isometric exercises** — not physical jerks, but using muscle pressure against fixed objects. Holding the sitting position, unsupported with your back against a wall, arms out in front of you, is good for skiers — and hard!

★ **Do not smoke** — between 120 and 130,000 people die of cancer every year in Britain. Smoking is one of the principal causes. Even if you are over 18, drink in moderation.

★ **Eat healthily** — cut down on fatty, starchy foods (especially if you are overweight). Eat fresh fruit, vegetables and lean meat or fish instead. Cut out sweets, crisps and chips.

Training for skiing

When you are skiing you use most of your body's major groups of muscles. That is why skiing requires so much energy – leg, trunk, neck and arm muscles are all needed to maintain your balance and hold you in the correct posture.

Strength, stamina and suppleness

First of all you need **strength** for skiing. Strong muscles, especially in the legs, not only help you ski well, they also protect your joints. The best way to build up strength is to apply the overload principle.

If a muscle is overloaded, the fibres will break down and then repair themselves, becoming stronger in the process. Training with weights (see below), spring pulleys, or simply by lifting and pulling your own body weight, are all good ways of developing strong muscles.

Stamina is the ability to make a big physical effort, recover quickly and repeat the effort. Stamina is endurance by the whole body, not just by a few muscles. To develop the kind of stamina that you need to ski well all day, you should work hard at your circuit training, which should include exercises like sit-ups, press-ups and burpees (squat thrusts).

Finally, skiing demands a great deal of **suppleness** – flexibility in the joints. Training for strength only, can restrict the range of movements in your joints. For this reason you need to include flexibility and mobility exercises in your training circuit.

Warming up before training

Warm muscles work more efficiently than cold ones, so always warm up before doing any exercises. (And remember this when you arrive cold and slightly stiff every morning to take the first ski lift). Warming up helps you to avoid torn muscles and strains. Three to five minutes is enough warming up time.
★ **Running on the spot** (1-$1\frac{1}{2}$ mins);
★ **Swinging the arms** (1-$1\frac{1}{2}$ mins);
★ **Shuffling** or running sideways (1-$1\frac{1}{2}$ mins).
If you have a rope, **skipping** is also good for warming up.

Strength and stamina circuit (10-15 minutes)

Here is a list of exercises that are good for the legs, trunk arms and shoulders. Choose two for each part of the body, making sure that you include some that are multi-purpose, for instance, squat thrusts which are suitable for legs, arms, shoulders and trunk.
★ **For the legs** – step-ups, squat thrusts, squat jumps, single leg squats.
★ **For the trunk** – sit-ups, trunk lifts, lateral raising, front lifts, squat thrusts.
★ **For the arms and shoulders** – press-ups, pull-ups, reverse arm press-ups, squat thrusts.

In order to decide how many of each exercise to do, within the total time for the circuit, experiment to see what is the maximum number of any one of the exercises you can do at once. Divide that number by two for normal training. Test yourself every now and again to see if the maximum you can achieve has increased and add onto your normal training numbers accordingly.

When you have finished each circuit, note the time taken and the number of exercises you have completed. Try to improve your performance the next time. Use this circuit twice a week.

Above: *Single leg squats, good leg exercises for strength and stamina.*
Above left: *Squat thrusts, or burpees, good for legs, trunk, arms and shoulders.*
Left: *Trunk lifts.*

Suppleness circuit (5 minutes)

These exercises are designed to extend the range of movement in your joints. They are meant to be smooth, flowing movements. Avoid jerky or bouncy actions at all costs. Move each joint to its greatest normal extent – and then use some muscle effort to push it a little further. Aim to produce slow, rhythmical presses, at the extreme limit of free movement.
★ **Abdominal hip and thigh stretch** – six times, hold five seconds;
★ **Frontal stretch** – six times, hold three seconds.
★ **Hip and knee rotation** – 30 seconds hip; 30 seconds knee;
★ **Neck rotation** – for 15 seconds;
★ **Shoulder stretch** – six times, hold three seconds. Repeat this programme three times.

Left: *Thigh, hip and abdominal stretch.* **Right:** *Hip and knee circling. Both exercises are good for suppleness.*

Using weights for training

This is not to be confused with competitive weight lifting. Using weights of about 1-2kg (3-5lbs) is a useful way to build up strength and endurance.

Before starting a weight training schedule, make sure that you have reached a reasonable level of general fitness, by using the step test (see page 19) on yourself. Remember that in building up your strength, the number of times you do an exercise (repetitions) is more important than the size of the weight.

Warming up exercises (five minutes)

As with any training, a warm-up before you start is essential. Try these exercises for one minute each:
★ **Swinging your arms;**
★ **Side bends;**
★ **Trunk, hip and knee bends;**
★ **Upper body rotation;**
★ **Alternate ankle stretch;**

Weight training for strength and stamina

Select exercises to develop a particular group of muscles – squats, for instance, for legs, back and stomach muscles. The minimum size of weight you should use is 1kg (2.5lbs) and the maximum 8kg (18lbs).
★ **Find out the maximum weight with which you can manage to complete each exercise.**
★ **Use half that weight for training.**
★ **Complete each repetition as quickly as you can and note your time improvement day by day.**
★ **If your times are not improving, add five repetitions.**
★ **Start with short rests between each exercise and gradually reduce the time spent resting as stamina improves.**
★ **Eight to ten repetitions of each exercise is enough.**
★ **These exercises are good for skiing** – squats, side bends, sit-ups (with the weight behind the head), bench presses, straight arm pullovers.

Relative energy demands of sports

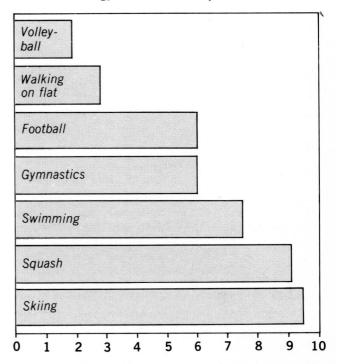

Sport	0 1 2 3 4 5 6 7 8 9 10
Volleyball	■■
Walking on flat	■■■
Football	■■■■■
Gymnastics	■■■■■
Swimming	■■■■■■
Squash	■■■■■■■
Skiing	■■■■■■■■

Safety with weights

Using weights can be dangerous if it is not done properly. So join an organised group with an instructor. Follow these safety points:
★ **Use the correct footwear** – tennis or jogging shoes.
★ **Use a mat** – to avoid hurting yourself on the floor.
★ **Check that the collars on the weights are tight.**
★ **Use chalk on the lifting bar so that it does not slip.**
★ **Lift with a straight back.**
★ **Keep your feet apart for good balance.**

Below: *Side bends with weights.*

Below: *Squats with weights.*

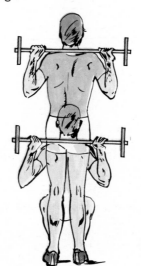

Below: *Straight arm pullovers.*

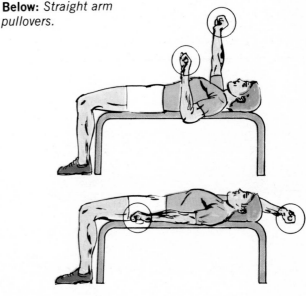

Ski clothing

Mountain weather can change dramatically in a few minutes — from sunshine to blizzard and from calm to chilling wind. When you are on the mountain you may be sitting still on a chairlift for a while, and a few minutes later skiing energetically down a steep piste.

To meet such a variety of needs, ski clothing must be tough, well designed and give the maximum freedom of movement. You will probably want it to be fashionable as well, but never choose cheap or glamorous clothes, if they are not warm and comfortable.

Your ski clothes should be made from tough, anti-slip outer fabrics. Shiny, smooth materials can turn you into a human toboggan if you fall on a steep slope. You need a strong zip, on the front of your anorak, as well as on each of your pockets.

Ski clothes keep you warm by insulating your body. Down-filled jackets are warmest of all, but they are expensive and suffer in the wet. Good quality, modern synthetic padding is cheaper, lighter, almost as warm, and washable. If you wear light weight garments or cheap padding, you will have to ski with many thick layers underneath, which is very uncomfortable. Several thin layers are better.

Jeans and tracksuits are a positive danger — they are not warm or protective. If you are well dressed you cut your risk of exposure and accident.

Your ski suit

This consists of a ski jacket, or **anorak**, and a **salopette**. The jacket should be made of warm, padded material, with a strong zip down the front and zip pockets. It should fit closely at the neck, cuffs and waist, to keep snow out. A high collar helps to keep your neck warm. Your jacket should come down 10-15cms (4-6ins) over the top of your trousers.

If you have an anorak already, which is no longer water resistant (it is not a good idea to have a waterproof one, which can make you hot and sweaty) you can buy spray-on proofer. If the sleeves of your anorak are not tight at the cuff, a narrow piece of elastic can be stitched into the lining, or the cuff itself, to make it grip round your wrist.

Salopettes are padded dungarees, made of the same anti-slip material as the jacket. They come up to your chest, and are held up by built-in braces. Make sure that your salopette covers your midriff and the small of your back (protecting your kidneys) and has wide shoulder straps for maximum comfort.

You will see ski instructors and some other skiers wearing **ski pants.** These are made of snowproof, stretch material. They fit tightly to the leg and are warm, comfortable and tough. But they are relatively expensive, compared to salopettes.

Below: *A sensibly dressed skier — missing only one thing — one of his skis!*

Under your ski suit

Warm muscles work more easily than cold ones and are thus less liable to injury. So skiers often wear tights (even the boys!), long johns, or even pyjama trousers, for extra leg insulation.

On a cold day the ideal number of top layers would be:
★ **a vest or T-shirt;**
★ **a cotton roll-neck sweater;**
★ **one (or perhaps two) lightweight woollen sweaters;**
★ **an anorak.**

Remember that several light layers are warm and more comfortable than fewer, heavy layers. Wearing nylon can make you hot and sticky. On less cold days a T-shirt and one cotton roll-neck should be enough under your jacket.

On your head

As you lose most body heat through your head, it is essential to wear a warm **hat**. Make sure it can be pulled down over your ears when necessary and that it is still windproof when stretched. In really bad weather the hood that should be attached to your anorak can be worn over your hat (kept on by your goggles), to keep snow out.

On your eyes and face

The glare of sunshine reflected off snow hurts your eyes, so you need **goggles** with tinted lenses. Goggles also prevent snow from blowing in to your eyes and even helps to keep your own spectacles on. Some types have interchangeable lenses for different weather conditions.

Sunglasses can be worn, but they come off and break easily in a fall. If they are not splinter-proof, keep them strictly for sightseeing.

The combination of bright sunshine and high altitude can give you more than just a good suntan — severe sunburn in some cases. Even on dull days you will probably need to wear **sun-screen creams** to protect your face, and especially your nose. People with delicate skins will need creams with a protection factor of at least number 6. The packet should tell you how much protection each cream offers, starting with the least protection at number 1. **Lip salve** to protect your lips is a good idea for everyone. Use only special lip salve for skiing.

On your hands

All skiers should wear **mittens** or **gloves** all the time, for warmth and to protect the hands. For beginners and skiers who still fall quite often, mittens are best, as they tend to be more waterproof and warmer.

Mittens can have vinyl palms and well padded backs. The cuffs should be long enough to leave no gap between your glove and jacket cuff. Avoid all-plastic mittens, which can leave hands sticky with perspiration without insulating them.

When you can ski really well, you could invest in leather gloves, or mittens and silk inners. In the meantime, good mittens are better than all but the best gloves.

On your feet

Under your ski boots you only actually need one pair of loop stitch **ski socks**. Wear them with thinner cotton socks

Above: *The complete outfit, including a helmet.*

underneath, changing the inner socks every day and the loop-stitch ones occasionally. Nylon socks can cause perspiration, chafing and blisters. Do not wear football or hockey socks.

Ordinary shoes are very little use on the icy, snow-packed streets of a ski resort. You therefore need some strong footwear for when you are not wearing ski boots. **Walking boots**, warm, lined **Wellington boots**, or the real thing, **après-ski boots**, have the necessary grip on the soles and are warm and high (to stop snow getting in). If you are going to a disco, wear your boots and carry your smart shoes to put on when you arrive.

Ski clothing checklist

Ski suit — anorak	☐
— salopettes	☐
Hat	☐
Goggles	☐
Protective cream	☐
Lip salve	☐
Mittens or gloves	☐
Socks — one loop stitch at least	☐
— one per day cotton or wool	☐
Boots for après ski	☐
T-shirts — two at least	☐
Cotton roll-neck sweater	☐
Woollen sweaters — two at least	☐
Tights, long johns or pyjamas	☐
Change of clothes for evenings	☐
Shoulder bag to carry shoes	☐

Boots, skis, bindings and sticks

Skiers of many years ago wore tweeds, knee socks and lace-up leather boots. Their boots were complicated to do up and offered little lateral support to the ankle, but they were quite comfortable for walking.

Nowadays, the reverse is true. Boot shells are made of rigid plastic, with simple **clip fastenings,** and offer maximum support. But they are not wasy to walk in.

These modern, colourful monsters are designed to hold your foot and ankle at exactly the right angle for skiing – with the knee bent slightly forwards. The soles of the boots are flat and infexible, so that they can snap out of a ski binding in a fall. Old fashioned, flexible boots would not work in modern bindings at all.

Boots have changed on the inside too. Today most have what are called **flow-fitting interiors**. The padding warms with the heat of your foot and after a short while takes on its exact shape. This makes modern boots very comfortable, as long as they fit properly.

Some of these flow-fitting interiors can be taken out of the boot, so when your boots are left in a damp, cold ski shed overnight, you can take the inners out and keep them warm and dry in your room. This makes putting on boots in the morning much easier.

Fitting ski boots

Most people hire their ski boots. But as you improve, boots will be probably be the first important item of equipment you will want to buy.

In either case you will be wearing recreational ski boots. These come up over the ankle and very often have a hinge that helps with forward movement, without allowing any sideways. The high, very stiff boots you see are for racing, designed for maximum support under extreme conditions.

The number of clips on a boot varies. Most boots have three or four clips, but some have only one. It is the specialist boots that tend to have fewest clips.

Here are a few simple rules to help in fitting your boots.
★ **Wear your ski socks** (one pair of loop stitch).
★ **With your foot in the boot and the clips open, tap your heel on the ground to make sure your foot is right into the boot.**
★ **Clip up the boot.**
★ **Wait a while for the flow-fit (if any) to adjust to your foot.**
★ **Tighten the boot again.**
★ **Your toes should be free to move,** but when you stand on your toes, your foot should not slide forwards inside, and your heel should not lift more than maximum 1cm ($\frac{1}{2}$in).

Boots that are too large can allow you to twist your ankle inside the boot. Boots that are too tight can cause cramp. Beware of boots with worn toes and heels – this can stop the safety mechanism of bindings working correctly.

When buying boots, take your time and fit them properly. Instant decisions can be regretted later. A good pair of modern plastic boots should give you many ski seasons of comfortable wear.

Above: *Well equipped skier traversing.*

Ski bindings

Good bindings, correctly adjusted, are what makes a potentially dangerous sport remarkably safe. Bindings are not part of the ski. They are a separate fitting, which clamps the boot and ski together, in such a way that as soon as the skier twists unnaturally or falls, the binding releases.

Bindings are adjustable according to snow conditions, and according to the height, weight, strength and ability of the skier. When you hire skis, the bindings are adjusted in the hire shop to fit your boots and your body weight. So, do not exchange boots or skis with anyone, unless the bindings are accurately readjusted.

Bindings should absorb minor shocks, so that they hold your boots and skis together tightly when you are going over bumps. But when you fall the heel should release upwards and the toe sideways. Check that **toe** and **heel pieces** of your bindings are opening and closing smoothly before you put on your skis. Clear any snow out of the bindings before putting your boots into them.

Always make sure that there is a **ski stopper** (ski brake) or **retaining strap** attached to each binding. If your bindings release, your skis must not run away (see page 39).

Above: *Runaway ski stopped by ski brake.*

Above: *Stepping into bindings.*

Ski sticks

Ski sticks are made of a light metal alloy, or steel, with a moulded plastic **grip handle** at the top and a **basket**, or plastic disc, at the bottom to stop the stick sinking deep into the snow. On the handle there is a **strap** to put round your wrist (see page 37).

Your sticks must be the right length, as you will use them all the time for walking, turning and balancing. If you put the tip of the stick on your ski and hold the handle, your forearm should be parallel to the ground.

Skis

Newcomers to skiing should always begin on hired skis. It is not a question of whether you can afford to buy skis or not. It is simply that when you start you will need shorter skis, which are easier to turn, and as you get better you will graduate to slightly longer ones. That is the moment to buy, if you are going to.

Hidden under the sleek outer lines of modern skis are many layers of materials like very hard polyurethane (for the top and bottom surfaces), wood, very often ash, or fibreglass (for the inner core) and steel (for the bottom edges). How each ski is made depends on what and who it is meant for — Ingemar Stenmark, or a six year-old beginner.

A recreational skier needs a relatively short ski (135-190cms depending on the height and skill of the individual), which will turn easily. A slalom or downhill racer needs longer and stiffer skis (175-210cms), which run faster and give him greater stability.

Skis for beginners should be between chin and eye height, although you may have to compromise if the hire shop has not exactly the right size.

There are several things you should check when you hire skis:

★ **Make sure there are no deep gouges in the sole of the ski.** Scratches are inevitable with hired skis. But real holes will stop the ski running smoothly. You can buy ski wax to help your skis to run well, especially on wet snow.

★ **Make sure that the edges are sharp.** Ski shops have machines to sharpen edges, so that the skis bite into the snow when you are carving a turn.

★ **Make sure that your skis have a definite camber.** This means that the ski is slightly arched when you are not standing on it. The ski flattens out when you stand on it and the effect of this is to distribute your weight evenly along its entire length. When your weight is momentarily off the ski as you turn, the camber helps the ski to grip the snow at tip and heel. A flat ski is a dead ski.

Weather and the skier

Ideal skiing weather would consist of bright sunshine every day, with light snowfalls overnight. But although conditions are often good, they are seldom perfect. And they can change very quickly in high mountains. A **storm** can blow up in less than hour, turning bright sun into a **blizzard; mists** rising from the valley can make the sky hazy, with **poor visibility**; low cloud can envelope the whole mountain in **fog**.

As you go up the mountain, the temperature drops, by 1°C for every 300 metres of altitude, or 2°F for every 1,000 feet. This drop in temperature as you go up is called the **lapse rate**. It means that even if it feels warm in the village it may be very cold at the top lift station.

If it is windy it is likely to feel even colder at the top of the mountain. This is called the **chill factor**.

In the thinner atmosphere of the high peaks, the sun too can be much warmer and more burning than it seems. In the sun your face can easily be **sunburnt**, while in the shade it may be below freezing. It is wise to wear protective cream whatever the weather, as unprotected skin can also suffer **wind burn**.

Blizzards and bad visibility

It is not always very cold when it snows, but watch out for a rising wind, which often brings a **blizzard**. If it is snowing hard in the early morning, the lifts to the top of the mountains will probably be closed and skiers will be discouraged from skiing anywhere but on the village nursery slopes.

If the lifts are open, but it is snowing lightly, remember that the snow will make your clothes wet eventually, even if they are proofed. **Wet clothes** are only ten per cent as effective as dry ones.

When visibility is very poor, the conditions are known as a **white out**. Sometimes white outs can be so bad that you cannot even see your skis!

Below: *Fog and low cloud can be dangerous to skiers.*

Above: *Summer skiing in a bikini — for experts only.*

In any kind of fog or mist it is very easy to get lost. You only have to miss one piste marker and you could go plunging over a cliff.

Bad visibility also means that it is very difficult to see bumps and dips in the ground, or to judge how steep a slope is. Without the contrast provided by sunlight and shadow, the white of the snow and the white of the cloud merge into one all-enveloping blanket, which can be very frightening.

If it starts to snow heavily, or visibility becomes poor:

★ **Head for home, or the nearest lift station** – study your piste map in advance, so you always know where you are and where to go.

★ **Keep together in a group** – you should not have been skiing alone, anyway. Stop frequently and make sure everyone is together.

★ **Yellow goggles can help** – change the lenses in your goggles to help discern the bumps.

★ **Ski very slowly** – feel your way, moving from one piste marker to the next.

The föhn

The föhn is a warm wind which can bring sudden changes of weather conditions to the Alps.

Air currents from the south cool as they rise up the southern, Italian side of the mountains. The clouds drop their moisture as rain (or snow) on the Italian slopes and then blow warm and dry air strongly down the northern slopes into France, Switzerland and Austria.

The winds can reach speeds of 130kph (80mph) and they have the curious effect of making people irritable.

As far as the skier is concerned the föhn melts the snow very quickly, making it sticky and thus difficult and sometimes dangerous to ski on. The sudden melting of the snow can also cause avalanches (see page 29).

The föhn usually brings extremely clear weather with it, making the most distant peaks stand out clearly. This may last for several days, only to be followed by snow.

Snow and the skier

Snow conditions vary with altitude, with sun and shade, with wind and calm, from one month to the next and from north facing slopes to south facing slopes. In fact there are so many different types of snow, that Alpine countries have many different words for it.

Most skiers remain on the prepared pistes, where the surface is packed firm by special machines, which also flatten out icy bumps. Until you are an advanced skier, you should not consider going off the piste without a guide or an instructor, who knowns the terrain. Never ski off-piste alone.

Skiing off-piste you will meet constantly changing snow conditions. One minute you could be in deep powder, the next in sticky, wet snow the consistency of porridge, which is known as *the leg breaker* in Austria.

If you study the chart below, you should be able to recognise most of the types of snow you are likely to meet, on and off-piste.

Type of snow	Characteristics	Causes	Skiing qualities
Piste	A pathway or route of compressed snow.	Made either by many skiers following the same route, or caterpillar tracked piste machines.	Excellent for all skiers, especially when the air is cold and dry. Always ski on the piste, unless taken off it by a guide or ski teacher.
Moguls	Mass of regularly shaped bumps on the piste.	Carved into steeper and steeper bumps as many skiers turn in the same places. When they become too steep usually flattened by piste machines.	Difficult for beginners, but great fun for better skiers. Demand strong piston action of the legs, using compression turns.
Wet heavy snow (Porridge or mashed potato)	Damp to touch, makes snowballs easily. Sticks to and clogs ski boots.	Snow falling in damp air at around zero, or when the temperature and humidity rises after a powder fall. Melted by direct sun or warm air.	Mediocre if surface only is porridge, but if complete snow cover is wet, very difficult and very dangerous to fall into. Avoid snow ploughing, as it is easy to catch an edge.
Ice	Smooth and solid, glass-like surface.	The rapid freezing of very wet snow, or snow in shadow, especially in late afternoon.	Very uncomfortable to ski on as it affords very little control. Causes falls and bruising, but seldom broken limbs, as skis do not stick to the surface during a fall. Put practically all your weight on the lower ski, edge your skis well and lean downhill. There may be soft snow above or to one side of an icy patch.
Tram-lines	Old ski tracks which have frozen solid.	Occurs often in late spring when tracks in soft snow freeze overnight.	Can be dangerous if skis become wedged in them; otherwise uncomfortable. Ski over them at right angles.
Crust (sun)	Shiny, roughened surface.	Snow cover melted and then re-frozen.	Breakable crust, which will not carry the skier's weight, is difficult and dangerous.
Crust (wind)	Dull, satiny surface; often lies in slabs which sound hollow when tapped.	When wind blows falling snow into lee drifts and compacts it.	Unbreakable crust, which will easily support the skier is quite difficult to ski on, but not otherwise dangerous.
Powder snow	Consists of very small ice crystals. Blows about like dust. Will not form snow balls.	Fresh snow falling in very dry air, without wind, at temperatures well below zero.	Excellent surface when lying up to 2ins deep on piste. Exciting challenge to experts when over 9ins deep. Powder is almost a cult in the American Rockies. Weight on the skis equally, or one will sink deeper than the other. No need to lean back until powder is really deep (12ins).
Spring or corn snow	Large, granular crystals, looks shiny from a distance.	Caused by the repeated melting and freezing of the snow cover.	Pleasant to ski when soft and not too deep, but difficult when either frozen solid in the early morning, or when in deep patches of sugar snow in between moguls. Time it right and it is perfect. Too early and it is still frozen; too late and it is mushy. Experts ski south facing slopes in the morning and north facing slopes in the afternoon.
Thin snow	Grass, roots or rocks can be seen through the snow surface.	Either by very light snowfall or sudden melting of existing snow cover.	Annoying to ski on as choice of descents limited, and difficult as objects just under the surface catch the soles of the skis, causing damage.

Safety on the slopes

Skiing used to be considered a dangerous sport. But today it is much less risky and the number of injuries is few (insurance companies estimate four per cent), compared to the large number of people who go skiing.

Modern boots, and bindings especially, offer a high level of protection against the most common ski injuries — twisted, strained or even broken legs and ankles.

Ski schools are now organised so that every skier in even the smallest resort can be taught to a nationally approved standard. The ski schools' teaching methods are constantly reviewed to make instruction better and safer.

Pistes, as ski runs are known, are maintained by resort authorities, using sophisticated machines, which grade and prepare run surfaces, packing down new snow, or even moving snow from where it fell to where it is needed.

Resorts have their reputation to uphold and therefore those responsible make sure that runs avoid avalanche tracks (avalanches usually follow well-known routes).

The rescue services are always on hand to deal with accidents. At the top of many runs, or discreetly tucked away in lift huts, there are special toboggans for use as stretchers, unattractively known as **blood wagons**. These are designed to be guided by one or two expert skiers, who can often dash to the village with an injured skier tied to the stretcher in less time than it would take to call up a snowcat or even a helicopter.

The **ski patrol** police the slopes and make sure that no one is left on the mountain after the lifts have closed at night. In almost every resort lift stations are all connected by telephone or radio to the base in the village.

The skier is his own worst enemy

Some accidents are inevitable, especially when there is a large number of people practising a sport which is new and unfamiliar to them.

Many newcomers to skiing will have made no effort to

Below: *A stretcher-toboggan used to carry injured skiers.*

Above: *Typical warning sign on the piste.*

train beforehand and are likely to be very unfit.

By far the highest proportion of accidents happen during free skiing (not in ski school) to people whose ambitions are greater than their skill. They either try turns that are too hard for them, or they try to be clever and go too fast. The speed merchants who shout, *"Achtung"* or *"Attention"* and expect everyone else to move out of the way are a danger to themselves and others. So are those who think that they do not need lessons, because they can slither down the mountain somehow.

What to watch for

★ **Some snow conditions can be dangerous.** Ice may seem alarming, but losing control on the ice usually means only a few bruises. The most dangerous type of snow is wet and sticky. Even if you are going slowly, a twisting fall in deep, wet snow can result in injury.

★ **The weather can be a hazard.** You should wear good ski clothing at all times to protect you against the cold.

★ **Keep to the piste.** It is possible to lose your way if you do not follow the piste signs, or do not know where to go in bad visibility.

★ **Beware — avalanche.** If you stray from the piste you could find yourself in an avalanche danger area. You could even set one off. One of the greatest ski teachers of recent years, Robert Blanc, was killed in an avalanche in 1980. Blanc invented Ski Evolutif, the method of learning on short skis and he pioneered the very successful French resort of Les Arcs. He was killed trying to rescue skiers who were thought to have been trapped in an avalanche — a tragedy made worse by the fact that the emergency call he answered turned out to have been a false alarm.

★ **Make sure your bindings are correctly adjusted.** This should be done in the ski shop, when you hire your skis.

★ **Always attach ski safety straps,** if your skis are fitted with them rather than ski brakes (see page 36).

Below: *Using a mortar to set off a controlled avalanche.*

Above: *Trains overturned by an avalanche at Zermatt.*

If there should be an accident

★ **Prevent further accidents by warning other skiers.** Plant a pair of crossed skis in the snow, uphill of the injured skier, to warn those coming down the hill.

★ **Keep the injured skier warm.**

★ **Do not move him or her,** unless it is absolutely necessary because they have fallen in a dangerous place, like a narrow gully or on the brow of a hill.

★ **Send two people off for help, while one stays with the injured skier.** Only an instructor, or a very good skier, should go off on their own to look for assistance.

★ **Make sure that you know exactly where the injured skier is.** Give the ski patrol all the information you can — mark the position of the accident on a piste map. Take note of the position of the nearest lift pylon, or other reference point.

The Skiway Code

It is just as important to observe a code of practice on the ski slopes as it is on the road. Like the Highway Code, the Skiway Code is a mixture of common sense, experience and good manners.

★ **The slower skier always has right of way.**

★ **Give priority to skiers downhill of you.**

★ **When you overtake slower skiers, pass uphill of them and as wide as possible.**

★ **If you fall on the piste or on the drag lift, move out of the way quickly.**

★ **Never walk on the piste.** You will leave deep holes in which other people could catch a ski.

★ **Look uphill to make sure the way is clear,** before moving off again after a stop or a fall. Do not stop in narrow places, or where other skiers cannot see you.

★ **Obey all warning signs.** *Fermé* (French), *chiuso* (Italian) and *geschlossen* (German) all mean closed.

★ **Keep clear of ski classes when you are skiing out of your own class.**

★ **Practise turning uphill to stop or slow down.** This is the safest and most effective method, useful in any emergency.

★ **Never ski beyond your ability.** If you are out of control, you are going too fast and too recklessly.

★ **Never ski alone.** Groups of at least four are best, one to stay at the scene of an accident, two to go for help.

★ **Learn the international mountain distress signal** — six regular shouts, whistles, or flashes of a light in a minute. The reply is three responses, with one minute before the next response.

Taking the ski lift

For the first day or two that you are learning to ski you will climb the mountain like the skiers of fifty years ago — on foot. Starting on flat ground, your class will gradually gain height as you acquire new skills, until everyone is rewarded with their first ride on a ski lift.

Drag lifts

The term **drag lift** covers a wide variety of tows that pull you along on your skis. In a few places this may be simply a long rope, turning round pulleys at each end. You grab it with your **gloved** hands and it pulls you gently uphill. These lifts are much more common in America than the Alps. The more comfortable, European version has little handles to hold on to.

For safety reasons every tow, no matter how simple, has an attendant. Do not try to use unattended lifts. There is usually a good reason why there is no one there. The lift may be under repair. It may be officially closed and about to be switched off. People have been known to spend all night stuck on chair lifts, because they jumped on just before the lift was switched off.

The commonest form of drag lift is the **button lift** (also known as the poma lift). If there is no rope tow in your resort, this will be the first lift you will use. This is how to ride the button:

★ **Put the straps of your ski sticks around one wrist.** You can do this before you reach the starting point. Do not forget that you will need one hand to grab the pole between the button and the cable, so put your stick straps round the other wrist.
★ **Position yourself at the bottom of the lift, with your skis parallel,** about 20-30cms (8-12ins) apart.
★ **Prepare to take the button from the attendant.**
★ **Bend you knees slightly to absorb the shock as the tow beings to pull.**
★ **Grip the pole of the tow with your thighs.** Do not sit on the button, as it will not hold you. It is only designed to pull you along. Take your weight on your legs.

★ **Balance over the middle of your skis,** letting your legs bend and flex to absorb the humps and bumps of the track.
★ **As you near the top, pull the pole down (it is on a spring) and disengage the button from between your legs.** Hold with your hand only until you are ready to let go.
★ **Step off the lift track sideways,** making room for the next person.

The other common type of drag lift is the **T-bar**. This is designed to take two people, side by side although it can be used by one person alone. This is how to ride a T-bar:

★ **Put your sticks in the hand that will be on the outside.** Your inside hand will be needed to hold the shaft of the T-bar.
★ **Stand in the line of the lift, skis almost together, and look over your inside shoulder to see when to grab the bar.**
★ **If the lift includes a downhill stretch, snowplough gently to stop yourself going faster than the lift.**
★ **At the top, decide which of you is going to hold the bar,** while the other gets off.
★ **Step out to the side of the lift,** making sure the bar has not caught in your anorak. Let go, and ski clear of the next person.

If you fall off a drag lift

Everyone falls off, sooner or later, so there is nothing to be ashamed of. If you are going up with your class, ask your instructor what he wants you to do if you fall off. He will probably tell you to wait at the side of the lift track, or perhaps to take off your skis, walk down and start again.

Whatever you do, if you fall off, get out of the way of the next person on the lift as soon as you can. Never walk down the line of the lift, your footprints could be dangerous to others, and **never** try to ski down the lift track.

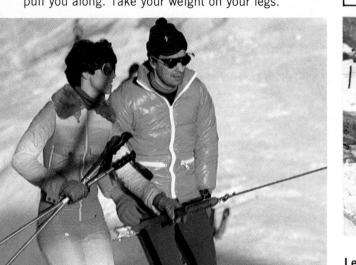

Left: *Riding a T-bar. These lifts are common in most resorts and can be used by one or two people.* **Above left:** *A lift attendant hands the button of a drag lift to a young skier.* **Above right:** *A drag lift with handles on it is often the first kind of lift beginners use.*

Chair lifts

Riding a chair lift is much easier than a drag lift. Chair lifts usually take you over unskiable terrain. A ten minute ride can be cold, but it will give you a marvellous view. But take care not to drop your sticks. You may never see them again. This is how to ride a chair lift:

★ **The attendant will indicate the spot on which to stand and wait for the chair.**

★ **Steady the chair with your hand as it comes up to you.**

★ **Sit down and keep the tips of your skis up,** to avoid them catching on the ground.

★ **Swing the safety bar and footrest (usually combined) down, in front of you.** Put your skis on the footrest.

★ **When you approach the last pylon of the chair lift, open the safety bar,** leaving your skis dangling.

★ **When your skis are sliding along the ground, push off, lean well forwards and ski down the slope provided,** away from the chair.

Above: *Preparing to ski down the slope, leaving a chair lift.*

Above: *A two-seater gondola lift. Skis are carried outside.*

Above: *Mountain railway below the Matterhorn.*

Cable cars and mountain railways

In large resorts and for really long ascents, there is often a **cable car**. Some modern cable cars are giants, capable of carrying over 200 people at a time. Other mini-cable cars are called **gondola lifts,** carrying only two or four people each time. In some places there are **bucket lifts** — which are just what they sound like, large buckets, in which two or more people can ride at a time.

In some of the older resorts, like Chamonix and Mürren, which pioneered the sport of skiing, there are **mountain railways**, driven by cog-wheels on a toothed track, or by cable.

III. Collecting your equipment

When you arrive in your resort, one of the first things to do is collect your equipment from the hire shop. If you have not brought equipment with you, you will be provided with a pair of skis, with bindings attached, a pair of boots and ski sticks.

The most important items of your equipment are your **boots**. They must be warm and comfortable and give you the support necessary to control your skis. Loose boots will rub and give you blisters; tight boots may cause cramp. Do not expect ski boots to be as comfortable as shoes. They are meant to hold your ankle rigid.

Many modern boots have what is called flow-fitting interiors, which mould to the shape of your foot. The flexible plastic lining will be cold and rather hard. Do up the clips loosely, making sure they are on the outside of each boot. After a few minutes, the heat of your foot will have warmed the interior of the boot and you will be able to tighten the clips.

Do up the clips in the order shown in the diagram below. Start with the clip on the instep of your foot. When you put on your boots it may help to tap the heel on the ground, so that your heel sinks firmly into the back of the inner boot.

When your boots are fastened your heel should not lift more than 1cm ($\frac{1}{2}$ inch). Try standing on your toes; your foot should not slide forwards inside your boot.

Right: *The inside of a typical ski hire shop.*
Below: *Do up the instep clip of your boot first. Then the toe clip, followed by the ankle clip and last the top clip. You may have to tighten them later.*

Skis and bindings

It may seem that there are thousands of different types of skis in the hire shop, and indeed there are many specialised models. However, all manufacturers make skis for hire and you will probably not be given a great deal of choice. Where you may be offered a choice is in the length of ski. Most beginners find that compact skis, which are slightly shorter than usual, and only come up to the chin, make learning easier. Therefore, if this is your first ski trip, opt for skis between chin and eyebrow height.

Attached to the skis will be the bindings, which are the essential link between your feet and your skis.

Safety bindings have to be most carefully fitted to your boots — and *your* boots only. So don't swap skis with anyone. The hire shop assistant will adjust the bindings so that they hold the ski firmly under normal conditions, but release at toe and heel under greater stress than usual. If they are too loose you cannot control your skis and if they are too tight they will not release.

If you have trouble with your bindings later on in your holiday, your instructor may be able to make some small adjustments to them, but it is always better to go back to the ski shop to have it done properly.

Below: *There are several ways of fastening your skis together so that they are easier to carry. Tie the safety straps together; use special rubber ties with a clip on the end; or lock the ski brakes round the skis.*

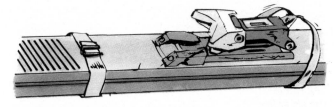

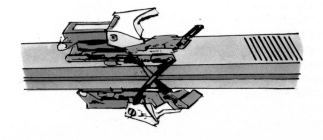

A new way to walk

Ski boots are not designed for walking — as you will feel the first time you try. To walk gracefully in ski boots takes a lot of practice. But if you leave the top clip undone, it is slightly easier. Be very careful walking on hard snow and ice. The soles of plastic ski boots do not offer much purchase. Try not to walk in boots too much as the tips of the toes and heels can wear away, leaving you with 'banana boots', which may not fit your bindings.

Your first experience of walking in ski boots will not be helped by the fact that you will be learning how to carry skis at the same time. Although you are more likely to be a danger to others with your skis, than to yourself. So, watch out you don't hit anyone with them.

There are several relatively easy ways to carry skis (and sticks). Put your skis sole to sole. Tie them with the retaining straps, or grip them together with the ski brakes. There are special rubber ties which you can use.

Hold the skis as upright as possible, tips down, tails up, balanced on your shoulder with the bindings just behind it. There will be times, in a cable car station for

Right: *Walking in ski boots is difficult to start with. Boots with hinges at the ankle allow some movement, but ski boots are meant to be inflexible. The flat plastic soles offer little grip on the snow. Carry your skis over one shoulder, with the bindings just behind your head and the tips forwards. Take care not to hit anyone when you swing round.*

instance, when you cannot put them over your shoulder, and you have to hold them close in front of you, upright.

Outside on the slopes, you can slide your ski stick straps over each end of your skis, carrying them like a suitcase with the poles of your ski sticks as the handle.

Off to the ski school

Every resort has a ski school. But finding it on the first day may not seem easy. Ski schools are usually on, or near the nursery slopes. These are the gentle, open snowfields, usually near the centre of the village, where people can begin safely. Nursery slopes should be away from busy, main pistes and preferably have a counter slope to stop run-away learners!

Because skiing is an important part of every ski country's tourist trade, most ski schools make sure that their instructors speak good English. Some may even be Brit-

ish. However, if they are difficult to understand this book will help to explain what they are trying to tell you.

All skiing nations have a ski instructors' association, which is responsible for training and maintaining standards. So, if your instructor is wearing a national ski school badge, he is well qualified.

From now on you will meet him, or her, every day in the same place with your group, who will all be of more or less the same standard. So make sure you know:

★ **Your instructor's name;**
★ **What the other members of the group look like;**
★ **Where and when you are to meet.**

Right: *The first place you will ski will be on the nursery slopes. These are often in, or near the village, like this slope at the Swiss resort of Morgins. Good nursery runs have gentle, even slopes, with a counter slope to stop runaway beginners. The office of the ski school will probably be near the nursery slopes. To start with you will probably meet your instructor and your class at the bottom of the nursery slope every day. Make a note of your instructor's name, remember where your class is to meet and what your class mates look like.*

Putting on skis

First, the introductions – find out the names of your instructor and the other members of your class, probably all beginners, like yourself.

You and your group will then find a piece of relatively flat ground and put on your skis. The flatter the area, the better, or you may find your skis escaping without you.

As it is, you will only be able to deal with one ski at a time. Put the other one on the ground, upside down, so that the binding acts as an anchor in the snow Push your sticks into the snow beside you.

The next thing to do is to make sure that there is no snow clinging to the bottom of your boot. Hard packed snow on the sole of your boot can prevent it from fitting into the binding correctly. Clean your boots by poking away the snow with a ski stick, or by scraping the sole of the boot on the edge of the ski.

Make sure no snow clings to the bottom of your boots, or blocks up your bindings.
Left: *Clear snow from your boot soles with your ski sticks.*
Right: *Or you can scrape the sole of the boot on your ski edge.*

Above: *To step into your bindings, first open the heel mechanism. Slot the front of your boot into the toe piece. Push down on your heel. The binding should close with a clunk.*

Left: *Find a flat area to put on your skis, so that they do not escape without you. Once on, always make sure that the safety straps are fastened. Many modern boots have ski brakes, making retaining straps unnecessary.*

Stepping into your bindings

Although there are many different types of bindings, the way in which you put your boot into them is always the same. First open up the heel mechanism. Place the toe of your boot into the front clamp of the binding, making sure it is clear of snow. Place the heel of your boot over the centre of the ski and push down. You should hear a reassuring clunk, as the heel piece closes, holding boot and ski firmly together. Now repeat the process with the other ski.

At this stage it is a good idea to check your bindings. Test that they release properly by feeling for the ball of one foot and then putting ever increasing pressure on it, kneeling forwards and sideways until the toe clamp allows your foot to break out of the binding. The heel should come out if you lunge forwards, lifting your heels. You can check the toe piece by hitting it sideways with the heel of your hand. If these checks fail ask your instructor to have a look at your bindings.

To release your bindings, when you want to take your skis off, either pull up the lever on the heel piece (to which the retaining straps are often secured), or in some cases there is a release catch which can be pressed with the tip of your stick.

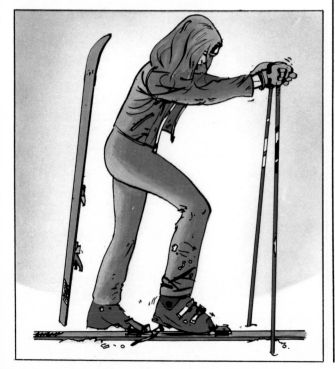

Left: *Some bindings release by pressing a button with a ski stick.*
Below: *When putting on skis, dig one into the snow and lean on your ski sticks.*

Above: *To judge the right length for ski sticks, stand with the tip on the floor, or on your ski. When you hold the grip, your forearm should be parallel to the ground, or floor.*

Left: *The correct way to use ski stick straps. Pass your hand upwards through the loop. Grip the handle with the strap between thumb and forefinger. When you press down, the strap should take the strain.*

The right length for ski sticks

Now that you are standing on level ground, with your skis on, pick up your ski sticks. You will see that they have short loops or straps hanging from the top of the handle.

You should hold your sticks, so that when you push down on them, the straps take most of the pressure, not your own hand grip on the handle. Pass your hand through the loop upwards from below, so that when you grab the handle the strap is against the grip, between your thumb and forefinger (see illustration above). Don't forget that the straps need to be adjusted to fit your hands with gloves on.

To judge the correct length for ski sticks, hold them with their tips on a hard floor (so that the tips do not sink in, making the sticks seem shorter). Your forearm should be parallel to the ground, making a right angle with your body.

Coping with skis

When skis are fitted with bindings they are also always fitted with either retaining straps, or ski brakes. If you take a tumble (as you surely will) your skis will sometimes come off. Your skis are designed to shoot downhill, fast. And that is what they will do, without you, unless they are stopped or tied to your feet.

Quite apart from the inconvenience of having to walk all the way to the bottom of the mountain to collect it, a runaway ski can cause serious injury (even death) to other skiers on the way down. Ski brakes (which dig into the snow) and retaining straps (tied round your ankles) can prevent horrible accidents, so never ski unless you have one or the other.

Left: *Runaway skis are very dangerous to others on the slopes. Therefore always make sure that your retaining straps are done up, as soon as you put on each ski. Many modern skis are fitted with ski brakes. When the boot is released from the binding, the ski brake automatically springs down and digs into the snow.*

Left: *Here are four different ways of getting the feel of your skis. Lean forwards, letting your boots and bindings take your weight. Now lean back. Then bend one knee and lift each ski in turn, tapping the tip of it on either side of the other ski. Bend your knee and lift the tail of each ski. These exercises will give you the feeling of the weight and size of your skis. Then lift your ski, keeping it parallel to the ground. Balance on the other ski.*

Left: *A ski class of children at the Swiss resort of Gstaad.*

Above: *An instructor teaching a line-up of young skiers.*

Getting to know your skis

At last you are on your skis, and the whole purpose of the holiday can begin. But by now, you are probably feeling trapped inside all your equipment and wondering how the racers on television make it look so easy.

They treat their skis almost as part of themselves. You too must become accustomed to the length and weight of your skis. To begin with just stand still for a little while and close your eyes. Think about your feet; feel your heels; move the pressure along the outside edges of your feet, until you are pressing on both your little toes. Now transfer your weight to the inside edges of your feet and try standing on the inside edges of the balls of your feet and your big toes.

Now relax. Let your knees sag forwards a little and distribute your weight evenly over the sole of your boots. During your long skiing career you will travel many thousands of miles. During your first week you may cover two or three miles. In some resorts experts can do 50 miles and more in a day! Soon you will forget you have skis on. But you will always be conscious of pressure placed on different parts of the foot, according to the techniques you use. This book will describe techniques by saying where the pressure should be. Becoming foot sensitive is an important part of controlling your skis.

Moving your weight round, you will have noticed how much support your boots give you and how your skis act as a platform, holding you up.

Using both sticks for balance, have a go at sliding your skis back and forth. Now try hopping both ski tails off the ground, landing gently. Now try tapping the front tip of one ski either side of the other. If you find this easy, try the same movement with the heels. These exercises will help you get used to your skis. You will very soon feel less awkward.

On the move

Not everywhere you go on skis is downhill. Often you will find that around the village, at the foot of the nursery slopes, and later on between lifts, you will have to walk on the flat in skis.

By now you will have discovered that if you walk normally on skis you will not go very far, or very fast. Try this instead: put your weight on your left ski; slide your right ski forwards; move your left arm forwards and plant your stick in the snow, level with the toe of your right boot; transfer your weight onto your right ski; repeat the process, starting by sliding your left ski forwards. Remember to keep your skis parallel.

As you walk, make sure that you lean forwards slightly. Don't plant your stick too far ahead, or you will not be able to put any purchase on it.

As you become better at walking on skis, build up a rhythm and slide a little way on each ski with each step. That way you will go faster. Look up, where you are going, and not at your feet.

Left: *Walking on skis is not easy. Slide each ski forwards in turn, pushing on the opposite stick. Lean forwards.*

Turning on the level — the clock turn

You can turn in a wide arc when walking along on skis, simply by stepping one ski out sideways with each pace. But you will find that in lift queues, in your ski school line up and in many other places, you will have to turn while stationary.

There are many ways of doing this — the most spectacular of which is the instructor's party trick of a full 180° turn in one jump. Your first stationary turns will be more painstaking! There are two simple methods of turning, which may seem awkward to start with, but which will soon become natural movements.

The easiest method is called the **clock turn**, because your skis leave an imprint in the snow like a clock face when you have turned (in soft snow).

When you are standing still, transfer your weight onto the tips of your skis by leaning forwards. Now step the tails of the skis round, one after the other, until you are pointing the way you want to go. For practice you can go right round, through 360°, facing inwards all the time. You can also turn the other way, stepping the tips round, as you face outwards.

Above: *Using the clock turn to turn round on flat ground is simple, but rather slow.*

Above: *Transfer your weight onto the tips of your skis. Step one ski tail out to one side.*

Above: *Step ski tails round alternately. Four moves should be enough to face the other way.*

Above: *A full 360° clock turn would leave a pattern like a clock face in the snow.*

Above: *Spectacular take off by an advanced skier.*

Turning on the level – the star turn

The **star turn** is a useful alternative, because you need much less space to do it in. Use the same movements as you used for the clock turn. Step your right ski tip round to the right. Then lean forwards and step your left ski tail to the left. By alternating like this you will soon be facing in the opposite direction. If you go right round through 360°, the pattern you leave on the snow will resemble a star, something like the Star of David.

Above: *A star turn is useful on flat ground, as it can be done in a limited space. Start with feet together.*

Above: *Lean back and step one ski tip round. Steady yourself on your ski sticks. Do not trip over them.*

Above: *Lean forwards, step the opposite ski tail round. Step tip and tail alternately.*

Above: *A full 360° star turn would leave a pattern like a Star of David in the snow.*

Stepping up the slope

Now that you are confident on flat ground, it is time to go uphill. To start with it will be your feet that carry you up the hill. Ski lifts are for later.

But you cannot just walk uphill. Your skis slide backwards as soon as the slope begins. So you have to dig your skis into the snow, so that they grip it. This is easier, if you understand a concept that will soon become second nature.

If you roll a ball down a hill, it will take the shortest route to the bottom. This most direct and steepest line from the top of a hill to the bottom is called the **fall line**. Every slope has a fall line. Look up at the mountain and imagine where the fall line runs, and how it changes as the slope alters.

The best way to make your skis grip the snow is to arrange them so that the edges are at right angles to the fall line, directly across the hill. Once you can do this you can stop yourself sliding back down again. And to go up, all you have to do is step up, as if you were going sideways up a very wide staircase.

Left: *Imagine that you are skiing straight down the mountain, taking the most direct route. The line you would take is called the fall line, an important concept for skiers. You seldom ski straight down the fall line, but many techniques require that you automatically know where it is. Edging your skis across the fall line means setting your skis on their inside (uphill) edges, at right angles to the fall line. Turning into the fall line means turning straight down the hill.*

Below: *Look up at the ski slopes on the mountain and try to imagine where the fall line is, on each part of the hill. It will not always be straight down, because the slope is never even. If you rolled a huge snowball down the slope in the illustration, it might take any of the paths indicated by the arrows. But every time it would take the line of least resistance. This is the fall line. In places you will find the piste follows the fall line and this is often where mogul fields are to be found.*

Sidestepping uphill

Sidestepping is a technique that you will use throughout your skiing career. It is the easiest way of going up a hill, especially a steep one.

The key to being able to sidestep, is being able to dig the uphill edges of your skis into the snow to form a shelf on which you can stand. If the snow is hard, you will find that very little of the sole of the ski is actually in touch with the ground.

In order to maintain the grip that your edges give you, and be comfortable, try pushing the top ski a little forward of the lower one and make sure that the majority of your weight is being carried on the ball of your lower foot.

If you feel that your lower ski is breaking away sideways down the hill, increase the angle of the ski edge by kneeling forwards and moving your thighs into the hill. Check that your head is directly above your lower big toe.

In order to keep your edges gripped into the snow as you sidestep up, concentrate on stepping from your lower big toe to your upper little toe.

You can use your sticks as supports either side of you, as you sidestep uphill. But ideally you should try to climb relying on your skis alone.

Left: *Sidestepping is the easiest way to go uphill on skis. Dig the uphill edges of your skis into the snow. The lower ski should make a firm platform on which to stand, while you move the upper ski uphill sideways. Then edge your upper ski and stand on it, while moving your lower ski up to it. Once you can go up, try going down. The key to sidestepping is mastering edge control, which is essential as your skiing improves.*

The herringbone step

Sidestepping is most useful for steeper slopes. Once you have mastered it, you can try the **herringbone**, a technique for moving uphill faster on gentle slopes.

Face directly up the fall line and open wide the tips of your skis, so that they make a very open V-shape. To grip the snow with your edges you will need to press on the big toes (the insides) of both feet. Now walk forwards up the hill, stepping from one big toe to the other. Take care not to cross your skis behind you, or to step on the baskets of your ski sticks.

Use your sticks for support by pressing against the top of the grip with the palms of your hands. Place the tips of the sticks directly behind each boot for maximum leverage.

As soon as the slope becomes steeper go back to sidestepping. And when you look back, you will see the V-shaped pattern left in the snow by your skis as you herringboned.

Right: *On gentle slopes the herringbone method is a useful way of going uphill. Face directly up the fall line, with your skis in a wide V-shape, tips apart, tails together. Make sure the tails do not cross. Grip the snow with the inside edges of both skis. Hold the tops of your ski stick handles in the palms of your hands. Push on the sticks, planted slightly behind you, and walk forwards uphill.*

Your first run

Now that you have climbed up the hill, all you have to do is turn round and slide down. That may sound easy, but to most people on their first day out it seems very difficult.

Your instructor will be there to help. He or she will have chosen a short slope (as little as 10 metres long) preferably with a flat run-out at the bottom, to slow you down.

Having climbed up the slope, the first thing to do is turn round. If you are not careful, gravity will hurry you off down the hill before you are ready.

Stand across the fall line. Turn your head and shoulders downhill. Plant your sticks as far down the slope as you can, shoulder width apart. Keep your arms out straight and put your weight on your sticks, held in the palms of your hands.

Now that you are supported on your sticks, start stepping your skis round. If the tips collide with your sticks, walk your skis backwards as you bring them round. When both skis are in the fall line, about hip width apart, your full weight will be on your sticks. This is called the **slope hang**. You are now ready to let go and make your first run.

Left: *Slope hanging is a useful method of holding yourself steady, while turning into the fall line. Place the butts of your stick handles against the heels of your hands. Take your weight on your sticks, planted downhill of you.*

Schussing

Running straight down the hill is called **schussing** – a word of German origin. If you are slope hanging at the top of a short hill, all you have to do is take the weight off your arms and sticks, change back to a normal grip on the handles, swing your sticks behind you, and you're off.

During the rest of your first day you will practise this again and again. You need to become quite proficient at sidestepping up the hill, turning on the slope (slope hanging) and then schussing down, while standing relaxed on your skis.

Remaining balanced while standing on moving skis is the next important thing to learn. Some people have better balance than others, so the time it takes will vary from person to person.

Your body moves very little in relation to your skis, although both you and your skis are sliding downhill. This is called dynamic balance and it is as important to you now, as it is to the ski racer travelling at 100kph (60mph) while hardly moving a limb.

At the beginning of each run, try to relax and feel that the entire sole of your foot is flat on the floor of your boots. To feel this, you will need to flex your ankles and knees a little, as well as your hips. Don't sit back, or stick your bottom out, even if you do feel as if you are about to sit down.

Carry your hands at hip height, forwards and a little away from your body. As soon as you get going your sticks should be pointing at about 45° downwards, and slightly outwards, behind you. Once under way you should feel more pressure on the front parts of your feet.

Developing your balance

As soon as you are beginning to feel confident at schussing, try some of these exercises, which will help develop it still further.

★ **Ski down the slope in the correct position and then hop,** so that the tails of both skis leave the ground.

★ **Ski down without your sticks and see if you can pick up your hat half way down.**

★ **Ski down looking up, or even to one side** (mind where you go), but not at your feet.

★ **Ski down, lift up foot, step out sideways,** transfer your weight to the foot you have just stepped out and bring the other alongside, so that you are now skiing parallel but to one side of the track you were on before.

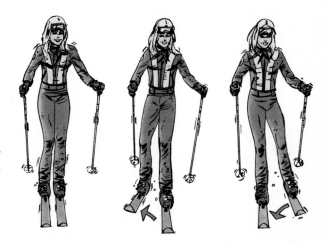

Above: *Improve your balance by stepping into a parallel track. Schuss, lift one foot, step out sideways, transfer your weight; other foot alongside.*

Below: *Two more balance exercises: Schuss down the slope, bending on the way down to pick up something like a hat; turn to look sideways.*

Left: *An instructor teaches a learner how to slope hang. He steadies her and stops her running forwards, while trying to persuade her to put her weight onto her sticks. The slope hang technique can be used to turn right round, through 180°.*

Above: *Once you are confident at schussing, try some of these exercises which will develop your balance. Ski down the slope in the normal schuss position. Then hop the tails of both skis off the ground. You should be able to land gently not losing balance.*

Falling down and getting up again

All skiers fall — even Olympic racers. Although a racing wipe-out may look spectacular, experts usually get up and walk away, even after coming unstuck at 120kph (75mph). This is because they know how to fall correctly — a technique that should be acquired by everyone.

If you fall properly you are less likely to hurt yourself. You will avoid twisting your knees and ankles which can be dangerous, even when you are going slowly. The third day at the slopes (just when you are beginning to feel confident) and the last day (when you are trying to get in as much skiing as possible) are the worst times for injuries.

If you feel yourself sliding into trouble, you can try to avoid a fall by opening up the gap between your skis. A wider base gives you more stability.

However, there will come a moment when it is better to accept that you are going to fall and do so gracefully.

The best way to fall is to sit down backwards and slightly to one side. And as you do so extend your legs forwards. This will prevent strain on your knees as your skis dig into the snow. Turn your skis across the fall line, so that the edges act as a brake. Keep your hands clear and your sticks behind you.

There will be times when you have no control over the way you fall and all you can do then is straighten your legs and remember that snow is not all that hard!

Above: *Try to avoid a fall by widening the gap between your skis, which gives you more stability.*

Above: *When you feel yourself falling, sit down backwards and slightly to one side.*

Above: *Extend your legs as you fall. This will prevent knee strain as your skis dig into the snow.*

Below: *Even the experts fall. Ingemar Stenmark, holder of two Olympic gold medals, crashes.*

Getting up after a fall

In the first few days you will fall over often. And you will find that getting up is one of the most exhausting parts of skiing. Eventually everyone works out a way of getting up that suits them, but this is the way that is usually taught by ski schools.

When you have collected your thoughts, gloves and hat arrange your skis below you and across the fall line. Make sure that the skis are edged into the hill, so that they do not slide away from you. Bring your body as close to your skis as possible, with your ankles almost touching your bottom.

Now with help from your sticks, or by pushing yourself up with your hand on the ground just uphill of your skis, roll yourself over onto your skis and stand up. If the snow is very soft you may have to push yourself up on your sticks laid flat in the snow.

Brush the snow off your clothes before you set off again. If you leave too much snow on your clothes it will make you wet as it melts. Wet clothes are not nearly as warm as dry ones.

Top right: *Every skier begins like this.*
Right: *In order to get up after a fall, arrange your skis across the fall line and below you. Edge your skis into the hill, so that they do not slide away from you. Bring your bottom as close to your skis as you can. Support yourself on your sticks. Then push yourself up onto your skis. If the snow is deep put your sticks flat on the snow and push up.*

Above: *When putting on skis on a slope, dig one ski and your sticks into the snow. Put on the lower ski first.*

Putting on skis on a slope

If you fall and your ski comes off half way down a run, it may be difficult to find anywhere flat to stand while putting it on again. However, it is quite easy to put skis on again on a slope.

Firstly, do not put your skis down and expect them to stay where they are. Remember how dangerous runaway skis can be (see page 36).

Dig one ski, tail first, into the snow, while you concentrate on the other. Dig your sticks in beside the ski — well within reach.

Place the first ski you are going to put on across the fall line, next to your lower foot. On a slope always attach your lower ski first. This gives you a secure platform on which to stand when putting on the second ski. At this stage it may help to lean on your sticks — one each side of you.

Always re-attach your safety straps (if your skis have them, rather than ski brakes).

Learning to snowplough

You can now climb up a hill, turn on your sticks and schuss down again. Every run so far has been straight down a gentle slope, with a flat area or counter slope, at the bottom to stop you.

Now you need to be able to control your speed, turn on the way down the hill and stop on your own, even on a slope. The best way to start is to **snowplough**.

The snowplough is the subject of many skiing jokes. It is often thought of as the poor relation of ski techniques. However, by learning to snowplough you also learn for the first time how to turn your skis and how to vary the grip of the edges on the snow, both of which are fundamental to all ski turns. The snowplough is therefore a very useful and necessary part of learning to ski.

Probably your first use of the snowplough will be to stop. But this is a habit that you should soon leave behind, except when going very slowly on crowded slopes. Even then do not do it too often, as it puts considerable pressure on your hip and knee joints. The best way of stopping is to turn your skis across the slope, and skid to a halt.

Some ski schools in France try to avoid teaching the snowplough altogether, by using very short skis which swivel easily on the snow. This makes turning your skis across the slope easy. But this method is now going out of style again, because it requires many expensive changes of ski length.

You will almost certainly be taught to make a snow-plough turn, and when you can do that you will quickly be able to stop with your skis parallel across the slope.

Below: *Even beginners and the very young can enjoy racing at their own standard. This boy is making a good snowplough turn. He is just beginning to transfer his weight onto his right ski (on the left in the picture) in order to turn to the left. Note the snow scuffed up under his righthand ski, as the inside edge grips the snow.*

Snowplough – the stance

Your instructor will probably take your group to a level place to show you the snowplough stance.

Your skis should be in a V-shape, with the tails wide apart and the tips close together – about 8cms (3ins) from each other. The skis should not be flat on the snow, but held on their inside edges. To keep them in this position, without being uncomfortable, bend your knees and lean forwards in much the same way as you do when schussing. Feel that you are standing on both big toes, pressing your knees ahead, along your skis, rather than in towards each other.

Try this exercise to help you adopt the right posture. Stand with your skis parallel, but slightly wider than hip-width apart. Stand tall, while feeling for the ball of each foot. Increase the pressure against your big toes. Kneel forwards slightly and imagine that you are stubbing out cigarette ends with each foot, swivelling your heels outwards.

The result of this will be that both your skis move out into a perfect snowplough, while you sink down slightly between them. You can try this exercise without skis or boots, in the hotel, or even before you go skiing.

Above: *An exercise to practise in order to improve your snowplough stance. Stand in the schuss position, then swivel your heels out. It is like stubbing out a cigarette.*

Gliding and braking

The next step is to do all this on the move – the **gliding snowplough**. Climb up your slope again. Turn into the fall line. Make sure that your feet are wider than hip width apart, you will need a wide base for stability.

Slide down the fall line for a few yards, feel for both big toes, press down and keep the pressure on. As your skis go out into the snowplough position you will feel more stable and as the edges of the skis grip you will have greater control over them, and thus over your speed.

As soon as you can control your speed, you are snowplough braking. When you are moving freely, stand fairly high, so that the inside edges do not bite. When you want to slow up, move back onto your heels and press out against your skis' tails. Feel the edges grip the snow?

Throughout your journey be aware of the pressure on your big toes, while keeping your upper body calm and relaxed. Keep your shoulders square on to your direction of travel. You should not move from the waist at all.

Right: *A gliding snowplough straight down the fall line, which need not be steep. This girl's feet are wide apart for extra stability. Her knees are slightly bent and her shoulders are squarely down the hill. She has a good, relaxed position.*

Left: *When you want to brake in a snowplough, lean back onto your ski tails and press out against the inside edges of your skis. Your knees should not touch — so do not ski with knock knees!*

Time to turn

By now you should be quite confident at holding the plough as you travel down the hill. Once you are able to move from the plough to the schuss and back again with ease, you can start to use your snowplough for turning.

Look at your skis as you plough directly down the fall line. What is each ski doing? Well, the right foot ski is pointing to the left and trying to go to the left. And the left foot ski is pointing to the right and trying to go to the right. Your skis are fighting each other, but as your weight is equally divided between the two, the forces exerted on each ski cancel each other out, and you go straight ahead.

If you were to help one ski more than the other, it would have its own way and take off in the direction it was pointing. The result would be to make you turn.

Try increasing the pressure on your left big toe, pushing your knee forwards (along the line of the ski, not inwards) and bring your head and shoulder over your left foot. Most of your weight will now be on left ski and you will turn the way your left ski is pointing, which is to the right.

Now move back into neutral (with your weight equally balanced on both skis), straighten up and try turning to the left. Remember to press against the inside edge of your foot. Keep you head over the turning ski.

Left: *A snowplough turn. Increase the pressure on the inside edge of one ski. Keep your head and shoulder over the turning ski. Repeat this going both ways.*

Below: *In many resorts you will be able to take a proficiency test at the end of your ski course. Here a ski instructor judges a young skier making a snowplough turn. Many ski schools award badges according to the level achieved by each skier.*

Freedom at last

Now that you can turn, the hard work is over. Your instructor will probably now allow you on a ski lift for the first time. No more walking up the hill!

The first type of lift you will use will be either a simple handle attached to a wire, or a button lift (see page 30). It will give you access to a long, wide and gentle slope on which to practise turns. If there is not much snow in the village you may take a lift to higher slopes.

At this stage it is easy to forget the basics, with the exhilaration of being able to ski freely. But look around at the better skiers for a reminder that you must improve your technique. You will see people keeping their skis parallel throughout turns — and that is what you can aim for. And you are not that far from it. Already you have learned about edging, change of pressure and angulation, all of which are essential for parallel turns.

Linking up your turns

The first step in beginning to ski like the experts is linking up your turns.

Increase your speed slightly. Stand tall as you ski down the fall line. Put pressure on one big toe and try to steer your ski round at the same time. Bend your knee forwards and don't forget to angulate. As soon as you feel yourself turning, straighten up again, weight evenly distributed onto both skis, and then turn the other way.

You will soon find that you can make one turn flow into the next. This is the way to develop rhythm in your turns. If you can steer the turning ski and make your turns rhythmical, you are ready to go further up the mountain, with your instructor, of course. But don't go too fast — you will tense up if you are frightened. Skiing out of control is dangerous to other skiers.

As soon as you feel confident at snowplough turning you can try a slalom course. Your instructor can set out a course in such a way that you will learn a lot by having to turn round a pole, rather than being able to choose where and when to turn. He will be able to place the poles where the shape of the slope (the terrain) can make the turn either easier or more difficult. And he can force you into making shorter or longer turns by changing the distance between the poles.

Left: *Linking up snowplough turns. In this diagram the green arrows indicate the amount of weight on each foot — heavy arrows for a lot of your weight and light arrows for little weight. The red arrows indicate the direction of travel. Start off (**above right**) with equal weight on each foot. Transfer your weight to the lower (in this case left) foot (**above left**) to turn to the right. Weight on both feet equally again (**far left**). Then transfer your weight to the lower (in this case right) foot (**left**) and turn to the left. Keep your head and shoulder over the foot that is turning. Steer your ski round each turn.*

Traversing across the slope

So far, wherever you go, across a slope or straight down it, your skis have been in the snowplough V-shape. But your aim is to ski parallel and the first time you will do this will be when skiing straight across a slope.

In both mountaineering and skiing terminology, travelling on a line across a slope is called traversing. When you traverse on skis you keep your skis on their uphill edges and parallel to one another, in much the same way as you did in sidestepping.

The inside edge of the lower ski is the foundation on which you stand, so make sure that the edge is biting into the snow firmly, so that it can carry the majority of your weight (see photograph, page 24).

You should be standing on the big toe of your lower foot and the little toe of your upper foot. Your skis should be about 20cm (8ins) apart and the upper ski about the same distance forward of the lower one. The steeper the slope (or the further apart your skis), the further forward the top ski must be, to allow your knees to bend evenly. Your head and downhill shoulder should be directly over your lower ski — angulation again.

You can easily tell if you are traversing correctly. On an even slope you should hardly loose height at all. You should be moving forwards and not slipping sideways.

Below: *A Swiss ski teacher leads his pupil down an easy traverse.*

Left: *Here are some exercises to help you improve and test your traversing.*
a) Find an even slope and traverse across it, lifting the tail of your upper ski.
b) Traverse and as you move across the slope step up sideways into a parallel track.
c) Traverse and hop the tails of both skis off the ground. Land as lightly as possible, on your edges. If you land with your skis flat, you will slip sideways down the hill. This can be useful (see side slipping, below).
d) Traverse and lift alternate heels off the ground.
The broad arrow shows the fall line. The steeper the slope the wider your skis.

Side slipping

In learning both to turn and traverse, you have been building up your **edge control** — making the edges of your skis bite into the snow and grip it.

As you become a more advanced skier, you will need to become more and more sensitive to the exact amount of edge needed for each manoeuvre. The better you control your edges, the better your skiing will become.

Side slipping is useful in two ways. Firstly, it is an easy way to take steep and difficult slopes slowly and safely. Secondly, it is an excellent way to practise edging your skis.

Begin by standing with your skis across the slope, as if you were about to traverse, but at right angles to the fall line, so you do not move forwards. Grip the snow by standing on the uphill edges of your skis. Move the top ski slightly forward of the lower ski. If your skis are edged properly, your knees should be pushed forwards and slightly inwards towards the slope.

Now, very slowly, roll your knees outwards, sideways down the slope. You do not have to move your feet at all. But you will find that with the edges released, gravity will pull your skis down the slope sideways.

When you have slipped a few feet, bring your knees back into the hill. This will set your skis on their inside edges again, making you stop. Repeat this exercise again and again, facing both ways.

You are now equipped to ski down some of the steep, narrow gullies that terrify inexperienced skiers. On any slope you consider too steep to ski, you can just side slide down a few feet at a time.

Left: *When your skis are edged, at right angles to the fall line, you should not slip sideways down the hill. If however, you release your edges, by rolling your knees outwards, you will slip sideways.*

Right: *Stop again by re-edging your skis, so that they grip the snow. Keep your sticks clear. Side slipping is useful both for negotiating steep sections of piste, which you do not want to go straight down, and also as a way to practise edge control.*

Skid into parallels

Now you can traverse easily and snowplough with confidence, all you have to do is link the two together.

Try to build up all the techniques you have learned so far, by varying your turns. Do a series of linked turns, then traverse, and then some turns linked both ways by a traverse.

By traversing with your skis parallel and using the snowplough for turns only, you can conserve energy. You can also travel faster. And because you are going faster you will find that you can modify your turns to make them more efficient.

The easiest part of a snowplough turn to modify is the last part. Begin your turn in the normal way by turning into the fall line. As you feel that the turn is happening,

lift and turn the tail of the inner ski and bring it parallel to the outer one and skid round the final few degrees of the turn, until you reach your new traverse line.

If you can do this, you have begun to ski parallel. You started the turn in the normal snowplough manner, by brushing one foot out into the fall line. But you finished the turn with a **skid,** having brought your skis parallel, half way through the turn.

Large bumps are good places to practise this technique. Traverse towards the bump. As you approach it push out the outer ski into the first part of a snowplough. Turn the inner ski parallel as you go over the bump. You will find that it is quite easy to do this and you will skid down the far side of the bump.

Below: *The first step towards skiing parallel is linking up a traverse, with the skis parallel, and a turn, using the snowplough.*

Left: *Begin with a snowplough turn into the fall line. When you feel yourself turning, lift the inner ski parallel to the outer one.*

Left: *As you complete the turn your skis will skid as they come parallel. Control your skid by increasing the edge on the outside ski.*

Right: *Large isolated bumps are the place to practise this. Draw the inner ski parallel as you go over the bump, and skid down the far side.*

Above: *The plough swing. Start in a high plough. Flatten the inner ski and pull its tail parallel to the outer ski. Steer both skis round the last part of the turn.*

The plough swing

The next important step is to make the second part of the turn without lifting your inner ski off the ground. Instead you must learn to keep both skis in contact with the snow (and so in control) and steer them round the turn.

Start by slope hanging, looking straight down the fall line of a gentle patch of piste. Slide off in a high, gliding plough. As soon as you begin to accelerate a little, flatten the left ski (which will be on the inside of the turn), if you want to turn left. At the same time tip your upper body forwards from the hips, straight down the fall line.

The effect of flattening the inside ski will be to make you go off in the direction in which the outer ski is pointing. And if you do that you will turn.

As soon as you have flattened the inside ski, pull the tail of it across the snow towards the outer ski, without taking any weight or pressure off it. Your skis will come parallel and will begin to skid. Control the skid by increasing the edge and pressure against the outer ski. You will also have to increase your angulation (see page 57).

Skidding both skis round the last part of a turn, without taking your weight off either of them, is called **plough swinging**.

Where to practise

The ideal slope for practising the plough swing is usually to be found on the beginners' **green runs**, or on the open gentle parts of **blue runs**.

Find a stretch of piste which begins with an even and very gentle slope, on which you can slope hang with ease. Below this there should be a short steeper section, perhaps as little as 2 or 3m (2-3 yards) long, which flattens out gradually.

Start your gliding plough on the first gentle part of the hill. Begin to turn as you reach the steeper section. Skid on the steepest part and traverse off onto the gentle slope below. Like practising on the bumps, this means that you will be able to skid when it is easiest, which is when you are going fastest.

Below: *Wide, open slopes, good for practising. The camera angle makes them look steeper than they are.*

Working towards parallels

Until now you have always begun your turns with a plough. The plough swing technique improved the second part of your turn, by bringing your skis parallel. Now it is time to improve the first, and more important part of your turn.

Begin by traversing with your skis about hip width apart. This is important for steering and edge control. Your skis should be on their uphill edges, as is normal in a traverse across the hill.

Now concentrate on changing the edge of your uphill ski — the one which will become the outside ski in the turn. Move your upper knee inwards, down the slope. This will flatten your upper ski and allow you to feel the inside edge coming into contact with the ground.

Once your upper ski is on its inside edge, press down on your upper big toe, as you move the ski out into a narrow plough. Extend your legs, and you will arrive in the fall line standing fairly upright. The remainder of the turn is as before — turning the inner ski parallel to the outer ski and skidding round the turn.

The process of changing the edges of your top ski, before you start the turn, is one of the most valuable techniques you will learn. You will still be using it as an advanced skier.

Above: *The first part of a parallel turn. Traverse with your skis about hip width apart. Change the edge of your uphill ski, moving your knee inwards, down the slope. Then press on your upper big toe.*
Below: *The ultimate aim — Phil Mahre of America, racing with the style that won him the 1981 World Cup.*

Basic swing turns

Now that you have improved the efficiency of both the beginning and the end of your turn, it is time to put the two together. The complete movement is known as a **basic swing turn**.

Your aim now should be to make the whole turn in one rhythmical movement, until you find it natural — at which point you will automatically begin to eliminate the plough part of the turn.

Here are the main points of the complete turn:
★ **Traverse with your skis hip width apart** (about 40cm, 16ins).
★ **Change the edge of the upper ski and steer it into a plough, while extending your legs as you arrive in the fall line, where you will be facing downhill.**
★ **Flatten the other ski** (which will be on the inside of the turn) by rolling your knee outwards.
★ **Then press down against the little toe of the inner ski** (edging it into the hill).
★ **Tip your upper body forwards from the hips straight down the hill** (angulation, see page 57).
★ **Steer your skis through a skid back into the traverse.**

What you need now is a long gentle slope where you can practise this time and time again. Ski as straight down the fall line as you dare; avoid traversing if you can. As soon as you have finished one turn, start another. Build up a strong **rhythm**. Put lots of effort into the beginning of every turn, concentrating on standing on your upper big toe.

Say (or even sing!) to yourself:
★ **Stand tall on your upper big toe;**
★ **Dive down the hill;**
★ **Change edges on the inner ski;**
★ **Skid into the parallel position.**
★ Stand tall on the upper big toe . . . (which will now, of course, be the other foot).

Linking basic swing turns, and developing them into feet-apart parallel turns, is not the only way of learning to ski parallel. But it is probably the simplest way to learn, once you have mastered snowplough turns.

As you improve, you will need to find a steeper slope and travel faster. This in turn will mean that you can make shorter linked turns, which will allow you to tackle still steeper slopes.

Above: *A basic swing turn. Extend your legs as you arrive in the fall line. Flatten the ski on the inside of the turn, tip your upper body downhill, skidding round the turn and back into the traverse.*
Below: *Plant your stick downhill and ahead of you.*

Pole planting

At this stage you can begin to use your sticks to help you turn.

Imagine that you are making a turn to the left. As you stand and press against your right (upper) big toe, plant your left stick downhill and ahead of you, about half way between your boot and your ski tip. Don't try and reach out too far and don't try to stab the snow like a life-long enemy.

Watch experienced skiers and you will see that pole planting should be a smooth, almost slow-motion action, which is an integral part of the whole turn. You can include the moment of planting the stick in your list of points to remember: stand on your upper big toe as you plant your stick; dive down the hill (removing your stick) by punching your fist forwards; change edges on the inner ski; skid into the parallel position (and prepare to plant your other stick).

Better parallel turns

Learning by steps and stages is bound to make you exaggerate your physical movements to start with. But gradually they will become faster and smoother until they are natural as walking or running.

If you are going to be a graceful and powerful skier you must be able to change your rhythm whenever you need to, and adapt your skiing whatever terrain the mountain offers.

Making better parallel turns is not just a question of going faster and more smoothly. It is being constantly on the watch for signals given to you in the behaviour of your skis.

When you change edges, it is sometimes a little easier if you take your weight off your skis for an instant. You can do this by sinking down before the turn, and then extending your legs quickly in what is effectively a jump without leaving the ground. This is called **up-unweighting**. Alternatively you can take the weight off your skis by tucking your legs up, so that you sink down. This is called **down unweighting** (see page 64).

As you improve you can experiment with both these methods. As you ski new runs you will find that it is easier to come up into some turns, and sink down into others.

In this way you can adapt your technique to the terrain and in so doing cut down your range of movements. This will make your skiing smoother and less tiring.

Left: *The first part of a parallel turn. Transfer your weight to your top ski while still in the traverse position.*

Right: *Change edges while still standing on the upper ski. Your upper body should dive down the fall line.*

Above: *Complete the transfer of weight to the outside ski. Keep your hips to the inside of the turn.*
Right: *Traverse out of the turn.*
Left: *As your parallel turns improve aim to reduce the amount you skid, as this cuts down your speed.*

Reducing the skid

Your next goal should be to control the amount of skid in your turns. Skidding means that you are travelling forwards and sideways at the same time. This makes learning to ski parallel easier in the first place, but it cuts down your speed.

Parallel turns without any skid are called **carved turns**, because the skis carve through the snow without any skid. Racers carve their turns with such good technique that they lose little or no speed while changing direction.

Any ski turn has three ingredients:
* ★ **Edging the ski;**
* ★ **Pressure on the edge**, to make it effective;
* ★ **Turning the ski** in the new direction.

When you start a snowplough turn, your skis are already edged and turned. All you have to do is add the pressure. The next step is to begin the turn in a snowplough and finish it by bringing your skis parallel, but you will know from this that if you begin with the turning ingredient, your skis will skid.

Therefore you have to revise the sequence and begin by increasing the amount of weight on your skis (pressing) and then edging and turning them. This will reduce your skid. The better the snow, the fitter you are and the better your equipment, the easier you will find it to **press, edge** and **turn,** and so reduce the amount of skid in your turns.

Right: *Improving your parallels: traverse with weight on downhill ski* **(top right).** *Plant your stick and stand on your top big toe* **(centre right).** *Turn into the fall line increasing pressure on outside ski* **(centre left).** *Back into the traverse, without skidding* **(bottom).**

Above: *Angulation is the way to increase the grip of your ski edges on the snow. Lean forwards from the hip with your head over the inside edge of your lower ski.*

Increase your angulation

Your ski edges are like the tyres of a car — they are the only means you have of gripping the ground. No matter how strong you are, or how powerful the car's engine, without the grip provided by your ski edges, or by the car's tyres, you and the car would slither around all over the place.

On gentle slopes at slow speeds this does not matter so much. But at higher speeds on steeper slopes you need much greater control, which only your edges gripping the snow can give you.

To give your edges maximum holding power, you have to **angulate**. Watch your instructor. When he is turning or traversing, he increases the pressure against his lower ski edge, by leaning outwards slightly from the hip. It is almost as if he is reaching out to someone downhill of him.

Imagine that you are skiing in a high, narrow plough. Your upper body and shoulders are facing down the hill. You release the edge of the inner ski and automatically turn, as the inside edge of the outer ski bites the snow. Your legs are now turned across the line of travel of your body. If you now lean forwards from the hip, so that your head is directly over the inside edge of your lower ski, your grip on the snow will improve enormously and you will be angulating.

Other ways to ski parallel

All national skis schools have different ways of teaching different people to ski parallel. The snowplough-into-basic-swing method is a slightly long way round, but it is suitable for almost everyone, regardless of age and fitness.

There is, however, another, quicker method for those who are agile and fit. It is called the **direct method** and some people find it gives quick results.

Imagine a production line that starts with a snowplough at the top of the hill and ends with a parallel at the bottom. It would be marvellous if it were that simple, and it is – almost.

Begin at the top of a long, gentle slope in a snowplough, facing directly down the fall line. Pick up some speed and begin making shallow, linked snowplough turns, never moving far out of the fall line.

Now each time you are facing directly down the hill start to spring lightly (without leaving the ground) from one big toe to the other. Establish a rhythm. Each time you come down, press against your outer big toe and

begin to turn your outer ski a little.

Maintain your rhythm, going up and down as you transfer your weight from one big toe to the other. Now reduce the width of your snowplough (the hill is not too steep, so you will not rush off out of control).

Spring from foot to foot with your upper body always facing straight down the slope. It should feel the same all the time, even when you have scrapped the snowplough completely and have your skis parallel throughout. And you have now reached the end of the production line hill. Go up and start again.

This time soften your movements. Don't exaggerate the way in which you spring from big toe to big toe. Make the turns slightly longer and plant your stick each time (see page 55).

When you can move from turn to turn without a traverse in between you are doing a form of short swing, which is what the experts do on the steepest slopes. With a short traverse between turns, you can now say that you are skiing parallel or are a parallel skier.

Right: *The direct method is a way to learn to ski parallel, which some people find gives fast results. Young people who are fit may find it better than the snowplough-into-basic-swing method.*

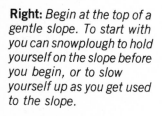

Right: *Begin at the top of a gentle slope. To start with you can snowplough to hold yourself on the slope before you begin, or to slow yourself up as you get used to the slope.*

Right: *As you pick up speed, begin to make shallow linked turns. To start with these will be snowplough turns. Start to spring lightly from one big toe to the other. Each time you come down, press against your big toe and turn your ski a little.*

Right: *To start with you will be making a short traverse between each turn. But your aim should be to move straight from one turn to the next. Establish a rhythm, springing from one big toe to the other.*

Right: *Open the tips of your skis by turning the inner ski as you press on the outer big toe. Eventually you will be able to keep your skis parallel, without a snowplough.*

Right: *Gradually make your movements softer, without exaggerating each turn. It will become easier if you ski a little faster, keeping your body facing directly down the fall line. Begin to make each turn longer, and plant your ski stick each time.*

Left: *The fan method is another way to learn to ski parallel that may suit people who find skiing down the fall line (however gentle), learning the direct method, difficult. Start in a shallow traverse and hop your ski tails down the slope. They will skid slightly, as you increase your angulation and re-edge your skis, steeering back up the hill.*

The fan method

If you want to try another way of learning to ski parallel, but find that skiing straight down the fall line, using the direct method, is a little too adventurous, then try the **fan method**.

Like many ski techniques, the name comes from the pattern that would be left behind if the exercise were done on virgin snow.

Start in a shallow traverse. Allow yourself to pick up some speed. Now hop the tails of your skis down the slope.

Try to land softly. As you land you will find that your ski (because they are not as purposefully edged as usual) will break away down the hill. They will skid slightly as you increase your angulation again, re-edge your skis and steer back up the hill. When you stop, you will find that you have taken a curved track across the slope.

You should practise this several times, going both ways. Doing everything to left and right is important, as many skiers find it easier to turn one way than the other.

As you become more confident, increase the steepness of your traverse and go faster. But fear not! Parallel skiing is an advanced technique and some speed is both necessary and helpful.

As you become used to going faster, you will find that soon you do not need to make a conscious hop at the beginning of the turn. A smooth extension of the legs is all that is needed.

By now your steep traverse will be close to the fall line. If you can make a fan-shaped turn actually starting in the fall line you are making good progress.

The next step is actually to cross the fall line. Slope hang on your sticks, facing the opposite way to your intended turn. Hop into the fall line, and then let your skis skid as usual through the rest of the fan.

When you can start not from a standstill, but from a traverse in the opposite direction, you will have completed your first parallel turn.

Compression turns

The suspension of a car is designed to even out bumps and dips in the ground, so that even though the wheels go up and down, the passengers remain fairly level.

The same applies to skiers — their legs should act as their suspension, folding up underneath them on bumps and extending into hollows. A good skier keeps his head, shoulders and upper body as calm and undisturbed as possible.

Being able to absorb the unevenness of the ground not only gives you a more comfortable ride, it also gives you more control. Try going over a little bump (not a big one) with your legs stiff. You will almost certainly take off. When your skis are in the air, you are out of control. You cannot stop or turn until your edges are once again gripping the snow.

Now relax and go over the same bump again. As the tips of your skis begin to rise up the bump, allow your legs to fold under you. Then as you go over the summit of the bump, push your legs down again. Your skis should remain in contact with the snow all the time.

Below: *A skier in the middle of a compression parallel turn. His thighs are parallel to the ground, which is correct.*

Above: *Absorbing the bumps with your legs gives you more control and makes skiing more comfortable.*

Above: *Your head should remain at the same level all the time. Let your legs act as your suspension.*

Above: *It is important to relax and as your skis rise over a bump, allow your legs to fold up under you. Extend them into hollows.*

Compression basic swings

Using this technique of absorbing bumps and dips while turning, results in what is called a **compression turn**. You will need this kind of turn all the time as you improve and take on the blue and red coded intermediate slopes. It makes skiing mogul fields fun instead of a nightmare.

You do not need to be a skilled skier of parallels to start on the bumps. You can use a variation of your basic swing technique.

Traverse across a slope and begin a basic swing turn — pushing the top ski out into a plough and turning into the fall line. At this point sink down, so that your thighs are parallel to the ground. Still squatting, bring the inner ski parallel to the outer ski and only when they are parallel should you push them out and away from you.

When you do push your skis away from you, you will find that you turn very quickly. Practise this until you can make the compression into a smooth, folding movement and the extension into a rapid, powerful one.

Right: *Compression basic swings are useful on moguls. Traverse and push out the top ski into a plough* **(top)**. *Turn into the fall line and sink down* **(centre)**. *With skis parallel, push out and away* **(bottom)**.

Compression parallels

A compression parallel turn has various names in various places. The French call it *avalement*, which means swallowing up the bumps; the Italians call it *assorbimento*, which means absorbing the bumps and the Austrians call it *wellen*, which means wave technique.

Traverse across the slope and again allow your legs to fold up under you, until your thighs are parallel with your skis. Make sure your skis are parallel.

Now roll your knees outwards, down the slope. As you do this, your edges will change automatically and you will begin to turn.

As you turn across the fall line, start to extend your legs again with a strong push, maintaining pressure against the edges to complete the turn.

You can practise compression turns on an even slope without bumps at first, progressing to moguls later.

Left: *Compression parallel turns are the expert's way of making mogul fields easy. Traverse across the slope* **(right)**. *Fold your legs up under you until your thighs are parallel with the ground* **(centre)**. *Roll your knees outwards, down the slope to change edges, and extend your legs with a strong push* **(left)**.

Coping with moguls

If you have been practising your compression basic swings, or your compression parallels, on a flat piste, now is the time to look for a real bump and test yourself.

If you do not wish to head straight for the nearest mogul field, find an isolated bump to start with. Approach it from the traverse. As your ski tips begin to rise over it relax your legs and fold them up beneath you. Try and judge when your feet are on the crest of the bump, for this is the moment you should plant your downhill stick (on the crest) and roll your knees downhill in order to change edges. Extend your legs as your skis skid down the far side of the bump. You may have to do this sharply, in order to keep your skis in contact with the snow.

You can make the turn easier by planting your stick and then turning your whole upper body to face directly down the slope. This is called anticipation, because it anticipates the direction in which you will be facing when you come out of the turn.

As you improve you will want to move onto a real mogul field and for this you will need to build up a strong rhythm in your turns, attacking the slope and thinking, **bend, turn, stretch** every time. You must also look ahead and choose a good line down through the moguls.

Below: *Practise skiing moguls on single bumps.*

Above: *Skiers can choose their line through moguls, turning on each bump or between each bump.*

Where do moguls come from?

At your resort, and in photographs of others, you will see that many of the steeper sections of piste are pock-marked with thousands of evenly shaped, domed humps. These are called **moguls**.

They appear because on steeper slopes skiers have to shorten and link up their turns in order to slow down. Every time a skier turns, he or she pushes snow up into a heap, which becomes packed solid and frozen into huge bumps.

Other skiers follow the same tracks, turning in the same places, and the bumps become even bigger. In some places, because of the shape of the ground, skiers have little or no alternative but to turn in the same place as everyone else, with the result that troughs become deeper and bumps bigger.

When moguls become too rough and high, piste maintenance men with tracked piste machines, called piste bashers, flatten them out.

Skiing the moguls can be very exciting, once you have mastered the technique of compressing your turns. Moguls were once considered as nothing but an inconvenience, but now there are even special competitions for skiing on them (see page 12).

Choosing a line

There are two keys to mastering the mogul fields. The first is the technique — retracting your legs, absorbing the bump, turning and extending your legs again — and the second is deciding where and when to turn.

It is best to learn compression turns on single bumps, or at most a small series of them. That way you do not have to travel too fast and you can concentrate on retracting and extending your legs.

Having learned the technique, you have now to cope with a mass of moguls and the fact that you will be moving much faster, as mogul fields tend to be steep.

You probably learned by turning on the actual summit of each bump. If you do this when skiing fast you will be thrown into the air and risk losing control. If you are good you can speed up your leg movements to cope with this, but it is much easier to choose the least difficult path through the bumps, which is not over the crests.

Imagine standing at the top of the mogul field and tipping a bucket of red dye down it. The water would snake down through the bumps, taking the path of least resistance. It would not run over the crests of the bumps, but in between them. This is the route you should take.

Skiing round the bumps you will still need to use your compression turns. But not going over the high spots means that you do not have to retract and extend your legs quite so far each time. This means that you can go as fast as the slope dictates, without losing control.

Right: *A Skier about to turn on the crest of a bump.*
Below: *An extensive mogul field.*

Advanced skiing techniques

When you stand on the bathroom scales, you can make yourself weigh more or less, according to where and how you place your weight. The girls may find this useful, when they have broken their diets, but everyone can use almost the same technique to improve their skiing.

If you are standing in the schuss position, and you bend your legs slightly, for a split second there will be less weight than usual on your skis. You can see this effect if you experiment with the bathroom scales. In skiing it is called **down-unweighting.** In contrast, if you hopped or extended your legs sharply, this would be called **up-unweighting**.

Unweighting your skis makes turning them easier. If there is less pressure holding your skis onto the snow, they will turn more freely.

In many ways this is a similar movement to that you learned for compression turns on the moguls, but with much less leg movement. Using parallel turns like this on the piste can be very useful. Although you unweight, your skis never leave the ground, so you can feel how much pressure there is on them throughout the turn.

If you are skiing in poor visibility you may not be able to see exactly what the snow surface ahead of you is like. By keeping your feet always in contact with the ground, you can feel out each bump. Unweighted turns can also be helpful on ice. By eliminating jerky movements, you can keep a better grip on the surface of the piste.

Right: *By bending or extending your legs sharply you can unweight (take the weight of your skis) for a moment. This makes turning easier.*
Below: *Fabienne Serrat, France.*

Short swings

Both racing cars and rally cars are built for high performance, but with different objectives. The same applies to skiing techniques. There are racing turns, like the step turn. And there are rally turns like **short swings** — particularly useful for descending narrow, steep hillsides, while keeping your speed down, so that you never lose control.

Short swings are linked parallel turns, with no traverse phase between each turn. What makes them different to other linked turns is the pronounced edge set at the end of each turn. This strong edging of the skis not only slows you down on a steep track, it also gives you a secure platform from which to make the next turn. Short swings are made fast, so that the sinking down movement at the end of one turn is in fact also the preparation for the next turn.

Your ski school instructor will probably not take you to the kind of terrain where short swings are necessary. But he or she will probably teach the technique, because it packages together all the important elements of advanced skiing. These are:

★ **Rhythm;**
★ **Leg turning** (and edge control, skis gripping the snow);
★ **Pole planting and timing;**
★ **Angulation** (no turning of the hips);
★ **Calm upper body and hands.**

Short swings — leg extension

There are two ways of approaching short swings. The first is to imagine a centre line down the hill. Keep your ski tips on the centre line and hop your feet first to one side and then to the other. As you do this, your legs will extend as you take off and compress as you land. Your ski tips should always be on the snow.

Short swings — leg retraction

This time place your feet on your imaginary centre line. As you plant your stick, retract your legs and lift both skis, so that they leave the snow. Turn when your skis are unweighted, and when you come down again, your feet should still be on the centre line. Short swings with leg retraction can be used on steeper terrain than is practical using leg extensions.

Below and left: *Short swings are very useful for descending steep, narrow hillsides, keeping your speed down, without losing control. They are fast, linked turns and there are two common ways of approaching them.*

Below: *Short swings with leg retraction. As you plant your ski stick, retract your legs and lift both skis. Turn when your skis are unweighted.*

Above: *Short swings with leg extension. Try to keep your skis tips running down an imaginary line, hopping your ski tails from one side of it to the other, by extending your legs to unweight your skis.*

Reading the mountain

The skilful skier moves about the mountain with ease and confidence. He does not get tired quickly and he always seems calm. How does he do it?

He is fit. He has sound technique, but he also understands, as a result of experience, which technique he should use where, which route to take and what conditions are going to be like on the route chosen.

Early in the day, he may ski down the middle of a mogul field but later on, when he is not so fresh, you may find him doing longer turns to one side of it.

He looks for shadows and expects the snow to be a little harder there, and therefore easier to turn on. In steep gullies, used by many skiers, he will not feel it is beneath him to side slip down the side, and so avoiding an icy base or slush. He will wedel, or link together lots of quick turns, when skiing down narrow trails, rather than use lots of energy ploughing. He will use a bump to turn on, or if conditions are icy, look for softer snow for turning.

The best way to acquire this knowledge is through experience — and that means lots of skiing. Concentrate on learning your technique from your instructor.

When you cannot be skiing, read ski magazine articles, practise on artificial slopes, talk to other experienced skiers. One of the best ways is to join a club. Many have technique talks and workshops at which you can discuss your experiences with others of the same standard.

Below: *Experienced skiers should know which technique is most effective on any kind of terrain.*

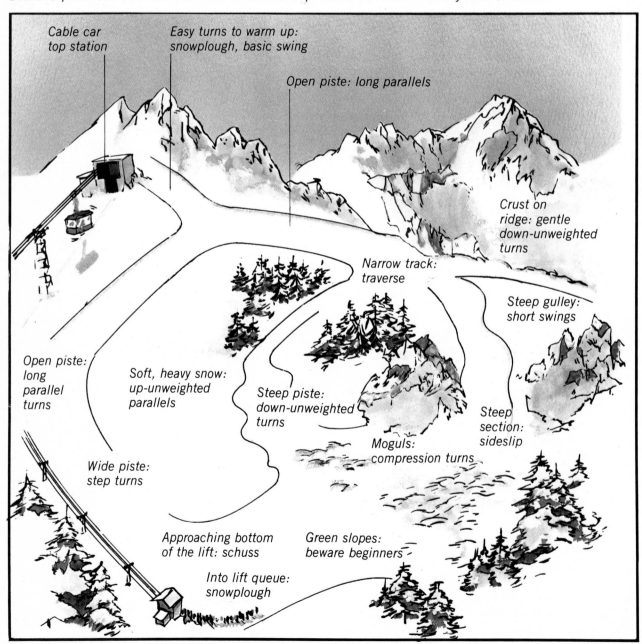

Cable car top station

Easy turns to warm up: snowplough, basic swing

Open piste: long parallels

Crust on ridge: gentle down-unweighted turns

Narrow track: traverse

Steep gulley: short swings

Open piste: long parallel turns

Soft, heavy snow: up-unweighted parallels

Steep piste: down-unweighted turns

Steep section: sideslip

Moguls: compression turns

Wide piste: step turns

Approaching bottom of the lift: schuss

Green slopes: beware beginners

Into lift queue: snowplough

Where to ski

Part of your skier's mountain craft is knowing what to expect on any stretch of piste. This will vary enormously.

The snow conditions chart on page 27 will help you to recognise most of the types of snow you are likely to meet and provide hints about the skiing qualities of each. The diagram below will help you understand where each kind of snow is likely to be found and why.

Conditions will vary, for example, according to whether the slope is in the sun or in the shade. Obviously you are more likely to meet ice on a cold, shady north-facing slope, than on a warm, sunny south-facing one. However, a sunny, high altitude slope may still be colder, with harder snow, than a shady, low altitide one, because of the lapse rate (see page 26).

You should also know where to expect conditions that might possibly be dangerous. Where two pistes cross, or a piste crosses the line of a drag lift, watch out for other skiers.

If you understand where you are likely to find which snow condition, you can choose the part of the mountain, and so the ski conditions, that you like best. In this way you can take full advantage of the range of skiing in your resort.

Below: *Skiers should know what snow conditions to expect wherever they ski.*

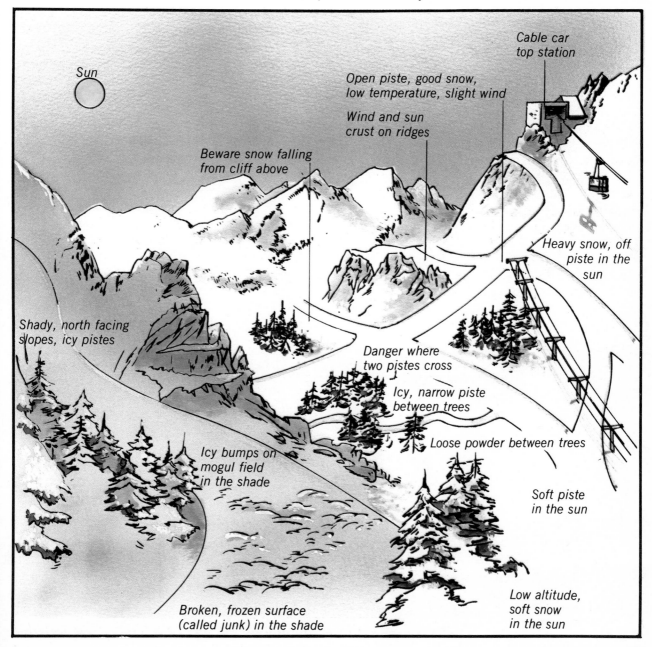

Powder snow and ice

The complete skier can cope with any snow conditions, including soft snow, or powder, and ice. As you improve you will want to venture beyond the piste into new, deep, untracked snow. Looking back up the hillside at the tracks you have left in virgin snow is one of the magic feelings of skiing well.

The term deep snow can mean anything from three inches to three feet. What is important to the skier is whether he can feel the base beneath the snow. If you can feel the base, your normal parallel technique will enable you to deal with soft snow. If you cannot feel the base you need a slightly different approach.

However deep the snow, you will immediately discover that you cannot see your skis — or that you can only see the tips. Now you will realise (if you have not understood before) why this book stresses the importance of feeling, instead of seeing, what your skis are doing.

The next thing you will notice is that your skis can feel almost trapped in the snow and that it takes a great deal of effort to change direction. This means both more muscle power and more speed.

It can be easier to turn if you use a more powerful leg extension at the beginning of the turn, or even jump round the turns if the snow is heavy. And the more courage you can muster to speed through the snow, the better off-piste skier you will be.

In order to maintain the high speeds needed, keep close to the fall line and build up the rhythm in your turns.

Keep your feet together and your shins will act as the bow of a boat — a bow wave of snow will build up round them. The effect of this is to slow you down, which makes it possible to tackle much steeper slopes than you will have skied before, without losing control.

You will also find that your skis grip more easily in deep snow, so you do not need quite so much edge, or pressure on the downhill ski. Instead put your weight evenly on both skis, so that one does not sink in further than the other.

Here are the main points to note in powder skiing:

★ **Ski faster,** more momentum for more turning power.
★ **Keep your feet together,** for bow wave resistence.
★ **More powerful upward movements in each turn.**
★ **Feel for your feet,** you will not be able to see them.
★ **Stand on both skis,** so that one does not sink too far.

When the powder is thigh deep, skiing becomes almost life flying. Your skis begin to plane through the snow like a speedboat through water. If this happens, of course you will not be able to feel the bumps — pretend they are there and still use the **bend, turn, stretch** technique of compression turns. Ski fast, keep turning, feet together.

Below: *When off-piste skiing you lose sight of your skis, so you must feel their movements.*

68

Above: *Skiing in untracked, powder snow.*
Right: *On ice grip the surface with your edges.*

Skiing on ice

You can come across ice anywhere, from a patch of well-used piste, to the surface of a glacier in summer skiing.

Nothing could be more different to deep snow skiing. Instead of feeling as if your skis are trapped by the snow, you will find it difficult to keep them in contact with it. You must ski with extremely accurate technique, simply in order to make your skis grip the hard, slippery surface.

If you meet a small patch of ice, you may be able to schuss across it and turn on softer snow below. However, if you have no choice but to ski on ice, the rule is not to disturb the contact between the ski edge and the ground. Avoid all jerky movements.

Start each turn by standing on the upper inside edge of your skis, so reducing the amount of skid. Angulate and keep yourself well balanced. Feel for the pressure on your lower or outside ski as you turn.

Sharp edges on your skis can be a great help when skiing on ice. Make sure the edges do not stand proud of the ski sole. Above all, do not let yourself be discouraged. Powder is the skiers's dream. Ice is the skiers' nightmare.

Techniques for racing

The ski racer aims to complete a course in the shortest possible time. This means taking the shortest possible route.

However, he must pass through each of the gates — flags in pairs set vertically, one above the other, obliquely across the hill, or horizontally side by side. He must also remain in control — if he loses his balance, he slows up or even falls.

To do this racers use a wide variety of turns, always looking for maximum efficiency. Some of the techniques used are not only good for slalom and giant slalom, they can also be useful to the recreational skier.

Two of these are the **step turn** and the **skating turn**. The step turn helps the racer to straighten his or her line of travel between gates. The skating turn is used to gain height or accelerate before turning. Both can be used by the recreational skier.

Right: *A typical slalom course, with gates, pairs of flags, which the racer must pass between. Some gates are set vertically, with the flags one above the other, some horizontally, with the flags side by side, others obliquely, with the flags across the hill. For slalom races the flags of each gate are set 4-5 metres apart. For giant slalom they are wider. A men's slalom course usually consists of about 75 gates, while women race through about 60 gates. The course is between 400 and 600 metres long.*

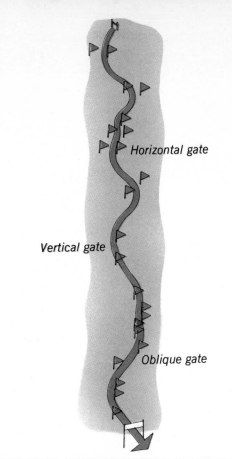

Horizontal gate

Vertical gate

Oblique gate

The step turn

This is a convenient way of moving uphill while skiing, and if necessary avoiding obstacles. It is a simple concept and easy to do when going slowly. At 30-50kph (20-30mph) it is harder!

Essentially, a step turn is nothing more complicated than a step to one side, onto a parallel track. If you are skiing near to, or straight down the fall line, you step out either onto a flat ski, or onto an inside edge.

If you are skiing in a traverse, step uphill on the outside edge of your upper ski. Then as soon as you have

transferred your weight, you change edges and turn. Take a look at the traversing step turn in detail:

★ **Traverse normally**, one ski slightly ahead of the other, knees slightly bent, angulate, weight on downhill ski.

★ **Step out and upwards with the uphill ski**, keeping it parallel to the lower ski.

★ **Straighten your legs**, transferring your weight onto the upper ski, bringing the lower ski up to it. You are now traversing again, but in a higher track

★ **Change your edges**, more angulation, skis together, turn.

Below: *The step turn — simple at slow speeds; difficult at racing speeds of 50kph.*

Left: *As you transfer your weight onto the upper ski, straighten your legs, change edges, angulate and turn.*

Above: *A step turn is simply a means of stepping sideways into a parallel track. Step onto the outside ski edge.*

Below: *Push off from the lower ski, onto your upper ski, which should be on its outside edge. Glide on the upper ski, before straightening up, and changing edges, and beginning the turn.*

Above: *The skating turn is useful for gaining height or accelerating before a turn. Bend your lower leg, pressing on the inside edge of the lower ski. Lift your upper ski out to change direction.*

The skating turn

Skaters and roller skaters use this technique to accelerate. If you are at a standstill on skates, with one blade set at 90 degrees to the other, you can push off from one and glide away on the other. Moving, you can do the same thing (almost like a sailing boat tacking), pushing off and gliding on alternate feet.

The same action on skis will produce the same result. This was once spectacularly demonstrated by the famous French skier Jean Claude Killy who made a film of his attempts to execute skating movements on skis.

The ski racer uses skating turns not only to take the straightest course through the bends, but also to accelerate. The recreational skier can use skating turns in the same way, but usually on fairly gentle slopes. When making a step turn from a traverse:

★ **Feel for the inside edge of the lower ski;**
★ **Bend your lower leg;**
★ **Point your upper ski out in the direction you wish to go** while . . .
★ **pushing off from your lower ski**, onto your upper ski which should be on its outside, upper edge;
★ **Glide on the upper ski**, straightening up before feeling for the inside edge of your upper ski and rolling your knee down the slope . . .
★ **changing your edges and beginning the turn**, now in a new track, because of the skating movement.

Right: *Skating turn by Malcolm Erskine, England Junior. Skating turns are useful in giant slalom. The skier should be as close as possible to each gate. A skating turn takes him into a new line, while also accelerating.*

Slalom, giant slalom and downhill

Ski techniques for racing are similar to those used by recreational skiers, but refined for maximum efficiency.

The first way in which a racer develops the effectiveness of a turn is by all but eliminating the skid. The second is in his choice of line down the course — a line that a recreational skier would probably not find possible because he lacks the combination of fitness, top class equipment, courage and experience, however good his technique under more leisurely conditions.

Slalom and giant slalom

Both these events involve negotiating a course made up of alternate red and blue flagged gates.

A World Championship course has a vertical drop of 220m (720ft) for men and 180m (590ft) for women. The gates are 4-5m (13-16.5ft) wide.

Men usually have to face about 75 gates and women about 60. The final number is decided by the course setter. In fact, both slalom and giant slalom are a battle between the course setter and the racer, as much as between the racer and the clock.

Each racer studies the course and chooses the straightest line down it, so as not to waste a second. At no point should the skier have to move his upper body in a way that might disturb the grip of his edges on the snow and make him lose speed.

To prevent himself from skidding, he will try and set his skis on their inside edges, well before he reaches the fall line, on every turn. This is something the recreational skier can also aim to do.

In addition, the racer not only angulates with his upper body, he also drops his hip and knee, angulating them as well in each turn. Racers keep their upper bodies as calm as possible, moving only hands and arms inwards to avoid the poles.

Slalom racers need good technique, and a great deal of agility — at high speed the gates seem very close together.

Giant slalom is similar to slalom, but faster and over a longer course — a vertical height difference of 400m (1,310ft) for men and 350m (1,150ft) for women. Giant slalom gates tend to be larger than those used for slalom, to be seen more clearly by skiers going faster.

Competitors make more rounded, carved turns in giant slalom, using more flexible skis.

Below: *Fine slalom technique by Perrine Pelen (France).*

Downhill racing

Downhill racing is the most spectacular of the Alpine disciplines and the most difficult to practise for. Most resorts do not have a course kept clear of other skiers, with safety nets positioned at possible danger points. Both these are necessary because downhill is, as its name suggests, a race for the fastest time from top to bottom.

A downhill course can have a vertical drop of 1,000m (3,250ft) and be 4km (2.5miles) long. Gates mark the edges of the course which competitors have to follow.

To achieve maximum speed, racers try to minimise the skid of their skis — a skid being a wasted, sideways movement. They also have to adopt the most aerodynamically efficient body position, cutting through the air as cleanly as possible.

In order to do this many of them wear one-piece cat suits, made of shiny material which offers very little air resistance. Even a racer's crash helmet is designed to improve the airflow round his body, although it naturally serves to prevent head injuries as well!

The **egg position** is the low crouch competitors adopt for maximum speed and stability, with their heads right down over their knees, hands and arms well forwards to allow their knees room to move. Apart from accelerating at the start (using the skating movement) and turning to follow the course, downhill racers try to keep to the egg position as much as possible, with their skis as flat as possible.

Another technique used in downhill is the **pre-jump**. It is easy to be thrown into the air by a bump — a fact well known to recreational skiers, who use compression turns to avoid it. Downhill racers take a small jump into the air, just before the bump, coming down immediately after it, rather than risk a larger jump, long in the air, and a heavy landing, which slows him down. It may not be possible to flex the legs enough to absorb a large bump when travelling at downhill racing speeds of 110-130kph (70-80mph).

Above: *Mark Rowan, one of the select band of World Speed Record challengers. He and others like Steve McKinney attain speeds of over 200kph (124.5mph) over a measured kilometre. To do so they use the egg position, like all downhill racers.*

Left: *The technique of pre-jumping is used by downhill racers to avoid being thrown too far into the air on bumps. By jumping slightly before the bump, the skier reduces the time he is in the air, and avoids a heavy landing.*

73

Artificial ski slopes

No one in Britain lives very far from a ski slope. There may not be many snow skiing areas, but there are now over 70 artificial slopes throughout the country. This means that everyone can ski, if they wish to.

Many of the slopes are owned by local councils and are open to the public. You can hire skis and boots, take lessons and become a good skier, before you even see a snow piste. In eight to twelve hours, from about £2.50 an hour, you can learn almost as much as you can in a week's ski holiday.

Artificial ski slopes come in all sizes. Some club slopes, or school slopes, are only about 20 metres long. The largest plastic slope in the country, at Hillend, just outside Edinburgh, is over 400 metres long. The largest in England, at Gloucester, is almost as big.

There are several different types of artificial surfaces for skiing. But the best, without doubt, is a plastic brush-like material called Dendix Snoslope. All major slopes, like Hillend, Gloucester, Rossendale, Sandown Park, Hillingdon and Pontypool are made of this. It consists of nylon bristles packed densely into stainless steel, criss-cross channelling. It is very realistic and has been compared to a piste of firmly packed snow.

Learning on plastic

The techniques used for skiing on artificial slopes are exactly the same as those used on snow. It is often an advantage not to have skied before, if you are going to learn on an artificial slope. Making the change from plastic to snow is much easier than from snow to plastic.

Learning on artificial slopes can be easier than learning on snow, because the plastic surface is always the same. Snow tends to change all the time, from ice one day to new snow, or slush the next. On plastic you can concentrate entirely on your techniques, without finding that a turn you mastered yesterday is difficult today, because the snow surface has changed.

If you just want to give skiing a try, without committing yourself to the expense of a series of lessons, you can ski in practice periods on most artificial ski slopes. But the best way to start is to do so properly, by learning with a qualified instructor.

Below: *Expert instruction is available at most of Britain's 70 or more artificial slopes.*

Find your nearest ski slope

While competitive skiing in Britain is practically all based on artificial slopes, you can ski regularly, without competing at all, if you wish. The best way to do this is join a ski club. Contact your Home Nation (England, Scotland, Wales or Northern Ireland) Ski Council to find out where the nearest club to your home is. The Ski Council's addresses are below. They can also provide you with information about coaching and proficiency tests. For a list of all the artificial slopes in Britain, write to the British Ski Federation.

British Ski Federation,
118 Eaton Square,
London SW1.

English Ski Council,
6th Floor, Area Library Building,
The Precinct,
Halesowen,
West Midlands.

Scottish National Ski Council,
The Loaning,
Meigle,
Perthshire,
Scotland.

Ski Council of Wales,
57 Exchange Buildings,
Swansea,
South Wales.

Ulster Ski Federation,
1 Darragh,
White Rock,
Killinchy,
County Down,
Northern Ireland.

Above: *Steve Dalton, a member of the British Freestyle Team, in action on the Pontypool artificial ski slope.*

Ski Tests

The British Junior Alpine Ski Tests are organised by the Home Nation Ski Councils. There are three tests: the **One Star Test**, which includes skills like side stepping, schussing, snowplough gliding and stopping, traversing and linked basic swing turns; the **Two Star Test**, including side slipping, basic swing or parallel turns, and a descent through six gates; the **Three Star Test**, including good parallel turns, short swings, and a slalom run of eight to 12 gates. All these tests can be taken on either artificial slopes or snow. There is also a series of tests for cross country skiers.

75

IV. Ski touring away from it all

Today's sport of ski touring uses skis as they were originally intended — as a means of transport. The hunters of Scandinavia used skis like this for thousands of years. But the rest of the world only began to take notice when Fridtjof Nansen, the Norwegian explorer, published a book about his ski-crossing of Greenland in 1888.

Nowadays ski touring is the fastest growing winter sport in America and not far behind in Europe. In German speaking countries it is called **langlauf**, in French it is **ski de fond**, and in Italian **sci da fondo**.

The many different ways in which it is possible to ski across country have developed into what are almost three different sports — **cross country skiing, Nordic touring** and Alpine **ski mountaineering**.

Cross country skiing is the most leisurely and the most popular type of ski touring. Using relatively cheap and simple equipment, this is a form of country walking in winter.

Most resorts now have signposted tracks through the best of their mountain countryside. The hills are not too steep. Provided that you can learn to walk feeling rather as if you had extra-long toe nails, you can cover ten miles a day or more, through fine forests in crisp air and bright sun, without lift queues and crowds.

Although some of the tracks may have been prepared, there is no such thing as a piste for cross country skiers. Their domain undulates across farmland and through narrow woodland paths. Cross country skiing is not for speed-mad piste bashers.

Equipment to match the terrain

To suit the type of skiing and the terrain, cross country ski equipment tends to be lighter than Alpine gear. The skis are narrower as well. This makes them much easier to handle, both on and off. The boots are more like training shoes, flexible and light. They clip on to the ski at the toe only.

This is the most obvious difference between Alpine and cross country skis and bindings. As the movement required is very like walking, the heel has to be able to

Below: *Ski touring, the skier's equivalent of country walking, is a fast-growing sport in Europe and America.*

Above: *Cross country marathons are popular. The Swedish Vasa race now has to be limited to 10,000 competitors.*

lift. For running downhill, the heel of the boot is fitted with a small pin, which fits into a plate on the ski.

The soles of the skis must provide some form of grip on the snow, because in cross country skiing you have to be able to go uphill, as well as down. Nordic hunters used to put animal skins on their skis. The grain of the fur allowed the ski to slide forwards, but not back.

Today experts use special waxes that have the same effect, but most people simply use skis with a pattern like a series of fish scales on the sole of the ski.

Cross country skis need to be slightly longer than Alpine skis. Ideally they should reach the wrist of your arm, when it is stretched above your head. The sticks need to be longer, as well. They are used for pushing yourself along, sometimes in deep powder snow, so they need to reach your armpit, when the tip is on the ground.

The powder snow on the forest tracks tends to cling round your calves and ankles, so you need gaiters or tight long socks. Above the knee, clothes can be as loose as you like, but not too heavy as cross country skiing can be warm work.

The basic technique of cross country skiing is similar to walking, except that each step is in slow motion, while you glide on the forward ski. You swing your arms high and rythmically, transferring your weight from one ski to the other. You use skating turns on the flat and stem turns downhill, although the latest fashion goes right back to the early days of Nordic skiing and the Telemark turn.

Marathon races

Needless to say, enthusiastic cross country skiers have not been content simply to roam round rural tracks. Cross country racing was well established long before downhill racing and some of the marathon races commemorate events far back in history.

The Vasa race in Sweden attracts 10,000 skiers every year. The race supposedly follows the route taken by Gustav Vasa (later King Gustav I) in revolt against the Danes in 1522.

The ultimate in cross country racing, the Olympic Biathlon, also carries memories of the Nordic hunters. The route is 20km (12.5 miles) long and includes four tests of target shooting. Appropriately enough the northern Europeans have always won this event, with two golds for Norway, one for Sweden and one for the USSR.

Skiing to the top of the world

Feeling adventurous? Do you want to ski way beyond the valley tracks and Alpine pistes? The Scandinavians have been crossing their own empty mountain regions on skis for generations. There are few snow-covered places that a good skier with the right equipment cannot reach. After all in 1970, one man, Yuichiro Miura of Japan, even skied down Mount Everest (8,847m, 29,028ft). He used a parachute and lost one ski part of the way down the western cwm, but he survived!

For those who want to visit vast fields of unpacked snow, follow glaciers and climb cols to uninhabited valleys, **Nordic touring** and **ski mountaineering** are the ideal sports. Parties travel on skis for several days at a time, self-contained with food, fuel and shelter, or on day-long treks between mountain huts.

Choice of techniques

The choice between the techniques of Nordic touring and ski mountaineering depends on the country to be crossed. Nordic touring calls for stronger and warmer versions of langlauf equipment and clothes, used where there are long distances to be covered, 30-50km (20-30 miles) a day, but with little actual climbing.

For those with a taste for real isolation, Nordic touring in the tundra of Lappland, in the Arctic, is a thrilling challenge and test of winter mountaincraft. A less extreme form of wilderness skiing can be found in the Jura mountains in south-eastern France, where there are miles of high plateaux and forests.

Climbers have often needed to use skis to reach remote peaks during the winter. But since on any approach to high mountains there is bound to be some actual climbing, ski mountaineers use Alpine ski equipment.

Even on the long traverses of the Alps, like the famous 130km (80 miles) High Level Route from Chamonix to Saas Fee, ski tourers spend much of their time on uphill sections, even carrying their skis and wearing climbing crampons on their boots.

Wherever skiers stray beyond the piste, the thrill of a lonely challenge against the wilderness carries serious potential dangers. No one must go ski mountaineering or Nordic touring unless they are very experienced skiers. Unless they are seasoned experts they take a guide, never travelling alone, but in small parties.

These are sports for well trained and physically fit men and women, provided with the best ski gear. Even then they face the usual dangers of the mountain environment — cold, exposure and avalanche.

Being inadequately clothed and cold soon leads to exhaustion. Even with good maps there is a danger of being lost, at high altitude, perhaps in bad weather. And then, as night falls bivouacing without a tent may be the least bad of a series of disastrous alternatives.

Ski mountaineering is the most technically demanding of the three forms of ski touring. For those who are well prepared, it can also be the most satisfying.

Below: *Nordic touring in the Swedish arctic.*

Above: *A group of ski mountaineers on an Alpine col.*

Conquering the Haute Route

In the summer of 1980 a group of seven students from Brynrefail School, Caernarfon, Wales, aged between 12 and 19, accompanied by three adults, joined the select band of those who have skied the famous Haute Route, from Chamonix to Zermatt. More than six months earlier they found themselves an experienced guide, John Ellis Roberts, who has done the High Route many times before. Then they trained, and trained, every weekend from Christmas to May: rock climbing, abseiling, skiing, map and compass theory and above all, physical fitness. Sponsors (principally Schools Abroad) helped with the considerable cost of the expedition.

Helped by a back-up team with a minibus they set off from Chamonix, reaching the top of the first cable car in a snowstorm. The one thing they had not been able to practise in Wales was using skins on their skis. After their first night in a mountain refuge they rose well before dawn to tackle the gruelling zig-zag climb to the Col du Chardonnet (3,323m, 10,900ft).

By this time everyone appreciated the rigorous training programme. The second day's journey to the Triente Hut was 11 hours long. The next day they found themselves on the treacherous Triente Icefall. They side-slipped and kick-turned until muscles ached. Then a gaping crevasse forced them to abseil down, one by one, before beginning the next ascent, to the Col des Ecandies, and so down to meet up with the back-up team at Champex. There they were forced to change plans, because a cable car was not running, and go by road to Fionnay.

A day of merciless slogging up tracks through avalanche debris was followed by a day-long, ten mile ski up the Otemma Glacier. The *gardien* of the Vignette Hut expressed anxiety about the ability of so young a team to make the next day's trek. But with two more cols, a narrow escape from an avalanche and 45km (28 miles) of solid skiing behind them they strode into Zermatt, proud to have achieved what even local experts doubted was possible.

Above: *The Welsh school group on the Otemma Glacier.*

V. Norse hunters and mad British

Some 4,500 years ago a man lost a ski in a Swedish bog near Hoting. It was dug up this century and found to be a metre long and 20cm (8ins) wide — pretty much the same dimensions as the latest innovation to the ski world, the Scorpian ski. The chances are that whoever wore the Hoting ski would have been perfectly at home on a Scorpian, binding it to his feet in the same place — 10cm (4ins) from the back of the ski.

Early cave drawings go back to the same period, both in Scandinavia and China, and show men on skis hunting with bows and arrows. One ski is usually long, of finger tip height from the ground, and the other shorter, at about one metre, or so. The men probably stood on the long ski and pushed themselves along on the short one, which had animal fur underneath to grip the snow. The action was similar to that of a child on a scooter, but left both hands free to wield a bow, or a spear.

The people depicted were known as *Skriddfinns*. The word ski is of Scandinavian origin and found in English in such words as *skid*.

Skiing to war

For centuries skis were mainly used for getting about on snow, and they were obviously used for tribal and then national warfare. In AD 1199 Saxo, the Swedish historian, mentions Finns on skis waging war, while in 1205 Norwegian soldiers skied to rescue King Haakon's kidnapped two-year-old son. This rescue is still commemorated every year in Norway by the Birkenbeiner crosscountry ski race. King Gustavus Adolphus of Sweden made extensive use of ski troops in his army and by 1820 they were an integral part of all Scandinavian armies.

Above: *The 4,500 year-old Hoting ski.*
Below: *A primitive rock carving of a hunter on skis.*

Above: *The rescue of King Haakon of Norway's son, 1205.*
Below: *A Scandinavian reindeer hunter on skis.*

The first ski competitions

Because man is a competitive animal, there would undoubtedly have been fierce competition as to who could ski the fastest or jump the furthest. However, the first recorded organised competitions were the Military Ski Games held at Christiania (now Oslo) in 1767. By the 1800s competitive ski events were firmly established.

The 1840s-1860s were the days of the great Sondre Norheim of Norway, who in 1860 jumped the then staggering distance of 30.5m (100ft).

In 1896 Matthias Zdarski established the first real Alpine ski school at Lillienfeld in Austria. He also invented a new type of leather strap binding (called the Lillienfeld binding), which was tightened at the heel by a clip. This was later modified and improved by another Austrian, Colonel Bilgeri. Zdarski was a great single stick enthusiast, and controversy raged for some years between the single and double stick brigades, until the issue was put beyond all doubt in the 1920s. Zdarski made the first methodical analysis of the stem turn and in 1905 held the first downhill ski race through gates, the results being judged more on style than on speed.

By the end of the 19th century, the sports of Nordic skiing and jumping were well established, using the Christiania and Telemark turning techniques. The Christiania was a swing turn, the body being swung, or jerked, in the desired direction. It was mainly used for stopping at the end of a ski jump. The Telemark was a steered turn with the outer ski acting as rudder, while the skier actually knelt on the inner ski. This is now becoming very popular again as a stunt in the USA, but it cannot be done with a binding that keeps the heel flat on the ski. That is why it virtually disappeared from downhill or Alpine skiing after the Kandahar spring cable became universal.

Above: *A Telemark turn, heel lifted, knee bent.*

Mad British skiers

At the end of the last century Sir Henry Lunn, who ran a travel agency, went to Norway and decided it would be a good idea to introduce skiing in the Alps. The idea caught on among British tourists, who were then bold, reckless and considered by all foreigners to be very eccentric. The Swiss in particular thought skiing would ruin the tourist trade of skating, tobogganing and curling. Cross-country skiing was unknown in Switzerland. In some places the mad British were pelted with stones, and things came to such a pass that they sometimes had to confine their skiing to moonlit nights.

In 1911 Lord Roberts of Kandahar, who was Commander-in-Chief of the British Army and a friend of Sir Henry Lunn, presented a cup for a downhill ski race; it was called the Roberts of Kandahar Cup. In 1928 the race was placed on an international footing and called the Arlberg-Kandahar. It was the blue riband of all downhill competition and such was its glamour that it gave birth to a whole host of ski equipment carrying the name Kandahar, the most famous of which was the spring cable binding.

During the 1914-18 war, many British prisoners escaped from Germany to Switzerland, where they were interned — usually in large mountain hotels. Having nothing better to do, they spent their winters skiing. On their return home at the end of the war they did much to popularise the sport in Britain.

Above: *Cartoon of Lord Roberts, Kandahar Cup founder.*
Below: *Start of the first slalom ski race at Murren, 1922.*

Pioneering sport

The years between 1896 to the outbreak of the 1914-18 war were the pioneering ones for Alpine skiing, when it became established as a sport in its own right. Among pioneers such as Alpina, Eriksen, Haug, Bergendahl and Huitfeldt, stands out the English name of Vivian Caulfield. His book on skiing, which appeared before 1914, became a classic.

Foremost in the field were the British ski runners, whose expertise gave rise to some 13 years of British ski supremacy, from 1920 to 1933. This was highlighted by the fact that some Swiss ski runs had — and still have — English names: *Oh God!* (for its steepness), *Mac's Leap* and *The Bumps* in the Jungfrau region, for example.

The new international sport

British men and women dominated world ski racing in the 1920s and early 1930s, winning all the major championships. There was intense rivalry between famous skiers such as Bill Bracken and Christopher Macintosh, while foremost among the women were girls such as Evie Pinching and Wendy Sale Barker. In fact the girls were world champions until the outbreak of war in 1939.

There were two reasons for this British supremacy. Firstly, the British had a head start. Secondly the continentals did not regard Alpine, or downhill skiing as a serious sport. Only jumping and langlauf were admitted as Olympic events.

Above: *Christopher Macintosh, champion British skier.*
Below: *Bill Bracken, arch rival of Macintosh.*

Below: *Evie Pinching, top British skier in the 1930s.*

Above: *In early Alpine races all skiers started at once in what was called a geschmozzle start. Collisions were frequent. Races were held on untracked snow.*

Controlling the racers

In the early days all competitors started a race at the same time, in what was called a **geschmozzle start**. The first past the post was the winner. Collisions and disputes soon made it necessary for racers to go one at a time at one-minute intervals. Races were on untracked snow and entrants could find any way down they wished.

This eventually had to be stopped after the Inferno Race at Murren in 1921 when it was found that the Norwegians, born jumpers, were proposing a short cut for their team by leaping over a precipice. It was decided this would give them an unfair advantage and a flag control was introduced to stop them. Even in the 1950s, however, downhill courses were still quite flexible. Ludwig (Lucky) Leitner of Austria won a big race in Zurs in 1955 by paying some boys to put a thin strip of snow across a café terrace, thus cutting off a biggish corner. You can imagine the astonishment of the customers sipping tea and eating cakes, as he tore through their midst.

Eventually the tight controls of the modern downhill courses were introduced. Tight they may now be, but the present speeds of 130kph (80mph) plus are faster than ever before, and most courses are nothing but take-it-straight-with-an-occasional-bend on a vertical descent of over 1,000m (3,000ft).

International competition

The Continentals were soon hot on British heels. Ski schools were being set up throughout the Alps and ski movements analysed. The first of these schools was that of Hannes Schneider at St Anton am Arlberg in Austria. Schneider taught the Arlberg Technique, based on the snowplough and stem Christiania. The body was kept in a deep crouch, known as the Arlberg Crouch. Although extremely effective, it looked ungainly.

In 1934 Toni Seelos, of Seefeld in Austria, introduced the upright *Tempo-Schwung* (speed-swing) method. In the days of untracked snow on the race courses, people went faster with feet together than apart. Seelos's method included an upright parallel skiing position with feet together and a quiet upper body, basically the same approach as that used by all good skiers today.

Toni Seelos was perhaps the greatest skier ever. He was so good that he was not allowed to compete in the 1936 Olympic Games, at Garmisch in Germany, on the flimsy grounds that he was a professional. He would have swept the board. In these games the downhill and slalom were admitted for the first time. The downhill was won by Berger Ruud, of Norway, who also won the jumping.

By the late 1930s, however, France was the dominant ski nation and two young Frenchmen, Emil Allais and James Couttet, were its champions. Allais perfected a new and complicated technique he called *Ski français*. Boots were clamped to the skis with a thong some two metres long. The ski method was pure parallel, with no stem or snowplough allowed. Turns were initiated by jumping the heels off the snow (called a *ruade* or mule kick) and the upper body and arms were rotated excessively in the direction of the turn.

At the same time the Swiss were using a similar technique without the ruade; it included the snowplough, stem turns and stem Christiania, or stem Christie. This technique was known as the 'lean forward style with rotation' and was an excellent method in all kinds of snow.

Below: *The ungainly Open Christiania turn, 1928.*

Above: *Jean Claude Killy, three gold medals, 1968.*

The dominant French

The French system was all conquering, but unsuitable for the slalom, which was introduced for the first time in the 1936 Olympic Games at Garmisch at the instigation of Sir Arnold Lunn, British doyen of the ski world. In the 1950s a group of young Austrians were developing a new method called the reversed shoulder (*gegen Schulter*). Unexaggerated, it enabled the skier to come as close as possible to any control flag. Using this method, the Austrian Toni Sailer won three Olympic gold medals — for downhill, giant slalom and slalom — at Cortina in 1956.

The Austrian method remained supreme until the early 1960s, when a group of Frenchmen appeared on the scene, led by the future world champion Jean Claude Killy. They used a modified French method which still had a touch of rotation in it. In his early days Killy raced with his feet together and often fell. So his trainer told him to try keeping them apart; this resulted in three golds in the Grenoble Olympics in 1968. Killy made skiing with feet apart socially acceptable. Skis kept well separated give much greater lateral stability and also allow each leg to work independently.

Since the dominance of Killy, no single nation or particular technique has been supreme. Ski schools, however, have always tended to exaggerate racing techniques. Not only should the method be used, but it must be clearly seen to be used. This, in many ways stultifies the freedom of movement the champion has initiated. Racers and children ski the same way — naturally — and rarely the way that people are taught in the ski schools.

Always remember that technique is a means to an end and not an end in itself. There is only one correct ski position and that is the one that allows the skier to move instantly to another position.

New equipment, new techniques

The story of ski equipment is very much that of the chicken and the egg: which came first? The whole trend has been towards achieving improved results in racing. As speeds became faster and conditions altered, so equipment altered to meet the conditions, which in their turn were altered by the new equipment.

The equipment-buying public has also been persuaded – nowadays more than ever – to buy equipment far beyond the ski potential of recreational skiers, in the hope of improvement and following fashion. Much excellent equipment, still serviceable, is discarded long before it is worn out.

Traditional skis

In the 60 years or so from 1920, equipment has leapt from the age of the horse and buggy to the age of the silicon chip. In the 1920s skis, much the same as they had been for centuries, were often handed down from father to son. A pair of skis would certainly be expected to last 50 years. Most were long, heavy and unwieldy, carved from a solid log of hickory, or ash. The groove down the middle was deep to keep the ski running straight in the untracked snow. There were no steel edges and running

Above: *Swiss gold and silver medalist (1948) Karl Molitor, using typical Kandahar bindings and wooden skis.*

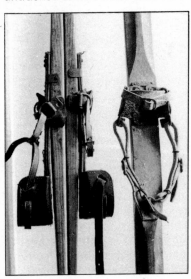

Above: *Two early leather bindings.* **Above right:** *Early clip boots, 1966.* **Below:** *Leather lace-up boots of the 1920s.*

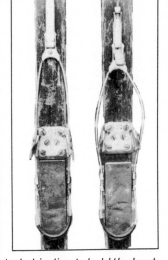

Above: *Walter Amstutz invented a binding to hold the boot heel to the ski.* **Above right:** *The Kandahar binding.*

soles were bare wood, needing constant waxing.

The skis were still strapped to the boots with leather thongs, basically little different from those used for hundreds of years. The boots were often just old army issue, with a couple of tacks driven into the heel to keep the binding clips from slipping off. Sticks were long and heavy and had huge baskets to prevent them disappearing into the soft snow.

Kandahar impact

As skiing increased in popularity and races became faster, it was important to keep the boot heel on the ski for better control. At first this was attempted by means of the Amstutz Spring (named after its designer Walter Amstutz, a famous Swiss skier).

However, the real watershed in skiing, the real birth of speed and technique, the greatest advance and single influence on it there has ever been, was the introduction of the Kandahar stirrup toe and steel spring cable, in the early 1930s. It is impossible to over-emphasise the impact of this binding and its effects on Alpine skiing. Apart from releasing the foot in a fall, no other binding designed since does anything different from the Kandahar. Its great contribution to skiing was to keep the boot and heel tightly in contact with the ski.

New and startling developments are round the corner, however. Electronic bindings, which monitor the pressure on the heel and toe, using microchip technology, are about to become available.

Skis too had to change to meet conditions on icy pistes, polished by ever-increasing numbers of skiers. There were no piste machines until the late 1960s. The first improvements were initially brass, and then steel, edges. These were followed by plastic running soles needing far less waxing. Skis were no longer made of solid wood but of thin strips of hickory or ash glued together (laminated), giving far more spring and control but a much shorter life – of perhaps only a year or so. In the 1960s wooden skis disappeared, to be replaced by either metal alloy or glass fibre surrounding a wood-laminated core, and finishing up as they are now – a mixture of all three.

Above: *Ski Evoltif pioneer, Robert Blanc, at Les Arcs.*

Shorter skis and higher boots

In the 1970s it was found that the new skis, with their improved running and control qualities, could be used much shorter and the era of the compact (eyebrow height) and mid-length (some 10cm, 4ins, above head height) skis began. Robert Blanc, at Les Arcs in France, started the Ski Evolutif method (called Graduated Length Method in the USA), introducing pupils to very short skis and gradually working upwards. The drawback was weaning them off the shorter skis. We have now finally come to the Scorpian, like the 4,500-year-old Hoting ski, one metre long, but made of aerospace grade carbon fibre.

The most important part of all ski equipment is the ski boot. It always has been. During the 1920s specialised leather boots were generally used, usually with a strap across the instep to keep the heel firmly down inside the boot. With some variations, they remained this way until suddenly, in 1959, new designs, higher up the ankle, were made to suit the new Wedeln (reversed shoulder) technique. During the 1960s boot laces gave way to clips and in the 1970s the early modern plastic boots replaced leather ones.

With skiing and ski equipment, there is only one thing you can be sure of: in ten years' time people will still be skiing but they will be using techniques and equipment that we have not yet dreamed of.

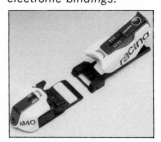

Above: *Gina Hathorn on Scorpian skis, the same size as the 4,500 year-old Hoting ski.* **Left:** *The reversed shoulder technique.* **Below:** *Marker electronic bindings.*

Ski history charted

Date	Event	Equipment	Technique	Remarks
4000BC	Invention of skis	One long, one short ski	Push and glide	Used for hunting and winter travelling
AD1500-1800	Jumping and cross-country racing start in Scandinavia	Long skis (above finger tip); three grooves in sole; one stick for cross country	Telemark and Christiania and kick turns	Hunting, travel and warfare
1800-1900	Serious sport in Scandinavia; sticks discarded on built-up jumps	Long skis with leather thong bindings	Telemark and Christiania kick turns	
c.1900	Lunns Travel introduces skis to Alps; popular in Austria	Long wood skis with leather thong bindings; one stick	Telemark, Christiania and kick turns	Skiing and skiers very unpopular with Swiss
1914-1918	British prisoners escaped from Germany, interned in Switzerland; practised skiing		'Dash and crash', plus inventive ski and available knowledge	Col. Bilgeri trains ski soldiers in Austria, invents new leather thong binding; Alpine war front between Austria and Italy; 40,000 men died
1920's	Skiing established as sport; included in 1924 and 1928 Winter Olympic Games, but only jumping and cross country (Nordic Combination)	Improved ski boots; metal edges late 1920s; also Amstutz spring bindings hold heel down for better control	Specialised and improved Telemark and Christiania; stem and stem Christiania turns appear; jump turns	British skiers supreme, teaching local instructors; many runs in Switzerland have English names; 1922 Murren: first slalom race—object, to simulate skiing down a slope with many trees
1930s	Skiing established in Switzerland and Austria; beomes world sport; downhill included in 1936 Olympics	Steel edges universal; Kandahar spring cable appears	Spring cable revolutionises technique; pistes appear as number of skiers increase	Start of Continental ski schools in Austria (under Hannes Schneider); also Swiss and French schools

The international sport

Date	Event	Technique	Ski Schools	Remarks
1920-1933	Main World Cup races established (jumping and cross country only) in 1924, 1928 and 1932 Olympics	British techniques supreme; no set pattern	First ski school organised by Hannes Schneider in Austria in 1931	Skiing still an amateur sport; races with 'geschmozzle start';
1934-1939	Downhill and slalom in 1936 Olympics; and skiing established as world sport	Seelos of Austria introduces speed-swing method	National ski schools spring up in Austria, France and Switzerland	British women still world champions in 1939; men's world ski supremacy passes from Austria to France in second half of 1930s
1945-1955	Era of rotation, which all racers use; 'Ski Francais'; 'lean forward with rotation' method used in Austria and Switzerland	French ski school supremacy, but Swiss school best for general skiing	National ski schools develop uniform methods; Stein Eriksen (Norway) originates reversed shoulder technique	Rotation method too clumsy for slalom; Austrians experiment with reversed shoulder method; racing controls still fairly elastic
1956-1966	Modern racing established; Sailer of Austria wins three gold medals at Cortina, 1956	Reversed shoulder method remains supreme	Austrian ski schools dominant	Heyday of Austrian skiing; schools develop method and make it static
1968-1972	World Cup circuit in full swing; Killy of France wins three gold medals at Winter Olympics, Grenoble, 1968	Feet-apart skiing appears in schools; more relaxation taught	British Association of Ski Instructors (BASI) achieves world recognition	Far less importance attached to position and far more to skiing naturally
1973-present day	World ski racing achieves mass audience appeal; Scotland becomes international ski racing area	Skiers initially taught with feet apart, with emphasis on mobility; but to ski upright with feet together still the criterion	Schools established worldwide; BASI can hold its own with any	Vast improvement in skiing standards worldwide; more ski than take part in any other sport; rapid growth of artificial ski slopes in Britain.

Left: *Norse god of skiing, Ullr.* **Centre:** *Swiss children demonstrate old-fashioned skis.* **Right:** *One of the first ski schools in Switzerland, 1934.*

New equipment, new techniques

Date	Skis	Boots	Bindings	Sticks	Remarks
1920-1930	Height: to extended finger tips; cut from one piece of hickory/ash; most villages had own ski carpenter; skis made to order; brass & steel strip screwed edges appear in 1927	Almost any – army, walking or mountain; often had nails in heel, over which leather binding was looped	Bilgeri-type metal stirrup with leather strap; Amstutz springs appear in 1927	Two cane sticks; big basket universal; often used as brake (stick-riding); made of bamboo/hazel, shoulder height	Cable cars open upper slopes to holiday-makers; heel springs give better control; stick-riding banned for racing in 1928
1931-1940	Height: to finger tips; laminated wood skis appear in 1935; steel edges universal; laminated skis have only short life; wood running soles need continual waxing	Specialised ski boots with ankle strap; boot is ankle height; each village has own bootmaker	Introduction of Kandahar spring cable binding revolutionises techniques in 1934; tight heel and clamped toe greatly increase risk of injury	Two cane sticks; big baskets for soft snow; shoulder height but, with rotation method, decreasing in length; metal replaces wood in 1939	Except for cable cars and mountain railways all downhills made after climb; equipment designed for soft snow runs; Kandahar binding greatest single advance in Alpine ski history; first drag-lifts appear in 1939
1946-1955	Height: reduced to wrist; solid skis out; screwed strip steel edges universal; plastic running soles appear in 1947 (less waxing); era of laminated wood ski	Laced leather boots ankle height; first stress on ankle support to control ski edges on new hard pistes	Kandahar spring cable and toe stirrup; French use long thong to clamp feet; much breaking of legs; safety cable heel release appears	Rotation technique needs very short, hip height sticks; metal universal; large baskets	Drag-lifts general, also chair lifts; pistes everywhere made by skiers after snow falls; Ski Club of GB lead drive for safety bindings
1956-1965	Height: up to wrist on extended arm; metal skis appear; also plastic with wood-laminated core; screwed steel strip edges	Higher leather boots for new wedeln method in 1960; clip boots appear and scorned, but established by 1965	Marker (Austrian) toe release with cable heel release in 1959; Kandahar toe stirrup disappears	As hard pistes increase baskets get smaller; sticks shoulder height again to suit new technique	Metal skis hold well on hard piste; yet thin profile good for soft snow; reversed shoulder technique in general use
1966-1975	Height: short ski (head height) appears in 1970; era of compact skis (about 15cm shorter); hidden racing edges displace screwed strips	High plastic boots appear in 1970, displacing leather	'Step-in' heel introduced; cable disappears except for touring; safety release now in several directions	Waist height, small baskets, metal and glass fibre; much lighter	Growth of ski industry; pistes prepared by snow-cats; schools advance to make skiing easier for holidaymakers; package tours spread
1976-present day	Compact head height skis used extensively by all skiers; mid-length skis appear in 1978; now combination of metal and plastic, often with wood core laminated in strips; shorter skis make skiing the Mogul fields far easier	Lightweight plastic boots introduced; fewer clips; more emphasis on comfort with flow-fitting inners	Step-in bindings universal; safety straps to prevent skis running away after fall give way to ski-stoppers	Small metal baskets, waist height; moulded grips; sword blade hilt appears	Appearance of ski-circus – interlinked ski lifts with miles of continuous pistes; all pistes prepared by caterpillar-tracked vehicles; ballet and aerobatic skiing established; mogul fields become ski speciality

French for skiers

Do you understand English, French?	*Comprenez-vous l'anglais, le français?*
Yes, no, a little	*Oui, non, un peu*
Good morning, good day, good good evening	*Bonjour, bonsoir*
Good night	*Bonne nuit*
Goodbye	*Au revoir*
Do you like dancing? Do you like skiing?	*Aimez-vous danser? Aimez-vous skier?*
I must be at the hotel by ten o'clock	*Je dois être à l'hôtel à dix heures*
Thank you	*Merci*
Excuse me	*Excusez-moi*
Where is the toilet please?	*Où sont les toilettes s'il vous plaît?*
One to ten	*un, deux, trois, quatre, cinq, six, sept, huit, neuf, dix*
Eleven to twenty	*onze, douze, treize, quatorze, quinze, seize, dix-sept, dix-huit, dix-neuf, vingt.*
Twenty-one, twenty-two	*vingt-et-un, vingt-deux*
Thirty to ninety	*trente, quarante, cinquante, soixante, soixante-dix, quatre-vingts, quatre-vingt-dix*
One hundred, two hundred	*cent, deux cents*
One thousand	*mille*

At the cafe, restaurant — Au café, au restaurant

May I have a . . . please?	*Pourrais-je avoir un(e) . . . s'il vous plaît?*
How much is . . .?	*Combien coûte . . .?*
Hot chocolate, coffee, tea	*Un chocolat chaud, un café, un thé*
Fizzy orange juice	*Un Orangina*
Flat water, mineral water	*Un Evian, un Vittel*
Soda water (fizzy)	*Un Perrier*
Slices of melted cheese eaten with potatoes, ham and gherkins	*Une raclette*
Cheese melted in wine, eaten with cubes of bread	*Une fondue savoyarde*

Cubes of best steak cooked in boiling oil accompanied by a variety of sauces	*Une fondue bourguignonne*
Apple/strawberry tart	*Une tarte aux pommes/fraises*
What time do you open, close?	*A quelle heure ouvrez-vous, fermez-vous?*

At the hotel — A l'hôtel

What time is breakfast, lunch, supper?	*A quelle heure est le petit-déjeuner, le déjeuner, le souper?*
Please may I have my key?	*Pourrais-je avoir ma clef s'il vous plaît?*
Room number . . .	*Chambre numéro . . .*
Have you seen the others from my group (our party leader)?	*Est-ce que vous avez vu les autres de mon groupe (notre chef de groupe)?*
My friend is coming later	*Mon ami viendra plus tard*
Please may I have a packed lunch	*Pourrais-je avoir un packed lunch s'il vous plaît*
Now, for tomorrow, early tomorrow morning	*De suite, pour demain, pour demain matin tôt*
I should like to take a bath/a a shower	*J'aimerais prendre un bain/une douche*

At the ski shop — Au magasin de ski

The boots, skis, sticks	*Les chaussures, les skis, les bâtons*
Too big, small, tight, loose	*Trop grand(e), petit(e), étroit(e), large*
Very expensive	*Très cher*
Please can you adjust my bindings?	*Pouvez-vous régler mes fixations s'il vous plaît?*
Do you have another pair of boots?	*Avez-vous d'autres paires de chaussures?*
They hurt, they are too tight	*Elles me font mal, elles me serrent*
I am a beginner, intermediate, advanced, a good skier	*Je suis débutant(e), moyen(ne), confirmé(e), un bon skieur*
I have come for the first third, fourth) time	*Je viens pour la première (deuxième, troisième, quatrième) fois*
The ski hat, the gloves	*Le bonnet de ski, les gants*
Sunglasses, goggles	*Les lunettes de soleil, les lunettes de ski*

At the souvenir shop — Au magasin de souvenirs

May I please have a postcard?	*Pourrais-je avoir une carte postale s'il vous plaît?*

How much is a stamp for a letter (postcard) to England?	*Combien coûte un timbre pour une lettre (carte postale) pour l'Angleterre?*
Do you have English books (papers, maps, guide books)?	*Avez-vous des livres (des journaux, des cartes géographiques, des guides) en anglais?*
An ashtray, doll, key ring, wallet (or purse), pendant, mug, jug, glass	*Un cendrier, une poupée, un porte-clef, un porte-feuille, (un porte-monnaie), un collier, une tasse, un pot, un verre*
Have you a smaller/cheaper one?	*En avez-vous un plus petit/moins cher?*

On the slopes — Sur les pistes

Take your sticks like this	*Tenez vos bâtons comme ça*
Copy me, do it like this, bend your knees, ankles, elbows	*Imitez-moi, faites-le comme ça, pliez les genoux, les chevilles, les coudes*
Upper body upright, stay upright	*Le haut du corps droit, restez droit*
Don't sit down	*Ne vous asseyez-pas (Ne t'asseois pas)*
Come one by one, one behind the other	*Venez un par un, l'un derrière l'autre*
More quickly, more slowly	*Plus vite, plus lentement*
Jump, lift one ski	*Sautez, levez un ski*
Keep your ski tips on the ground	*Laissez vos spatules à terre*
Touch your boots	*Touchez vos chaussures*
Put your weight on the lower ski	*Poids sur le ski aval*
Straight run, snowplough, traverse	*Schuss, chasse-neige, traverse*
Basic turn, parallel turn, sideslip uphill turn	*Virage de base, virage parallèle, dérapage, virage amont*
That's good, bad, terrible	*C'est bon, mauvais, catastrophique*
Please show me (us) again	*Montrez-moi (nous) encore une fois s'il vous plaît*
I have hurt myself	*Je me suis fait mal*
Uphill side, downhill side, uphill ski, downhill ski	*L'amont, l'aval, ski amont, ski aval*

The inside edge, outside edge	*La carre intérieure, carre extérieure*
Put your weight on the downhill ski	*Le poids du corps sur le ski aval*
Turn your shoulders, turn round	*Tournez vos épaules, tournez-vous*
The ski run	*La piste*
The ski lift, drag lift, chair lift the cable car, the mountain railway	*La remontée mécanique, le remonte-pente, le télésiège, le téléphérique, le funiculaire*
Top station, bottom station	*La station d'altitude, la station dans la vallée*
We meet at nine o'clock, half past nine, quarter past nine, a quarter to ten	*Nous nous retrouverons à neuf heures, à neuf heures et demie, à neuf heures et quart, à dix heures moins le quart*
The meeting place for tomorrow is...	*Le lieu de rendez-vous pour demain est...*
I have lost my group/ski teacher	*J'ai perdu mon groupe/le moniteur*
I am hungry, thirsty, frightened	*J'ai faim, soif, peur*
I am tired	*Je suis fatigué(e)*
I am cold, warm	*J'ai froid, chaud*
I must go to the ski school at ten o'clock	*Je dois aller à l'école de ski à dix heures*
Tomorrow there is a race	*Demain il y aura une course*
The prizegiving	*La distribution des prix*
To win a medal	*Gagner une médaille*
Bronze, silver, gold	*Bronze, argent, or*

At the first aid station, at the doctor's — Au poste de secours, chez le medecin

My foot (leg, arm, head, shoulder) hurts	*Mon pied (jambe, bras, tête, épaule) me fait mal*
My name is, I am called...	*Je m'appelle...*
My school is (is called)	*Mon école s'appelle...*
My home address is...	*Mon adresse personnelle est...*
How old are you?	*Quel âge avez-vous/as-tu?*
I am fourteen, sixteen	*J'ai quatorze ans, seize ans*
A sticking plaster, a bandage, a plaster cast	*Un sparadrap, un bandage, un plâtre*
The insurance	*L'assurance*
You must not ski for two days	*Vous ne devrez pas skier pendant deux jours*

German for skiers

Do you understand English, German?	*Verstehen Sie Englisch, Deutsch?*
Yes, no, a little	*Ja, nein, ein wenig*
Please speak slowly	*Bitte langsam sprechen*
Good morning, good day, good evening	*Guten Morgen, guten Tag, guten Abend*
Good night	*Gute Nacht*
Goodbye	*Auf Wiedersehen*
Do you like dancing? Do you like skiing?	*Tanzen Sie gern? Fahren Sie gern Ski?*
I must be in the hotel by ten o'clock	*Ich muss um zehn Uhr im Hotel sein*
Thank you	*Danke*
Excuse me	*Entschuldigen Sie bitte*
Where is the toilet (the exit) please?	*Wo ist die Toilette (der Ausgang) bitte?*
One to ten	*Eins, zwei, drei, vier, fünf, sechs, sieben, acht, neun, zehn*
Eleven to twenty	*Elf, zwölf, dreizehn, vierzehn, fünfzehn, sechzehn, siebzehn, achtzehn, neunzehn, zwanzig*
Twenty-one, twenty-two	*Einundzwanzig, zweiundzwanzig*
Thirty to ninety	*Dreissig, vierzig, fünfzig, sechzig, achtzig, neunzig*
One hundred, two hundred	*Hundert, zweihundert*
One thousand	*Tausend*

At the cafe, restaurant Im Cafe, Restaurant

May I have a . . . please?	*Kann ich bitte ein . . . haben?*
What time do you open, close?	*Wann machen Sie auf, zu?*
How much is . . .?	*Wieviel kostet . . .?*
Hot chocolate, coffee, tea, milk	*Kakao, Kaffee, Tee, Milch*
Orange juice, natural lemon, a soft drink	*Orangensaft, Zitrone natur, Limonade*
A mixture of orangeade and coca-cola	*Radler*
Cake, chocolate cake, apple strudel	*Kuchen, Sachertorte, Apfelstrudel*
Open sandwich with cheese, cold meat	*Käsebrot, Wurstbrot*
Frankfurters with bread, chips	*Würstchen mit Brot, Pommes Frites*
Gulasch soup, pea soup with frankfurters	*Gulaschsuppe, Erbensuppe mit Würstchen*
Bacon and egg, pancake	*Ham und Eggs, Kaiserschmarrn*

Fried veal in breadcrumbs, with salad	*Wienerschnitzel mit Salat*

At the hotel Im Hotel

What time is breakfast, lunch, supper?	*Wann ist das Frühstück, Mittagessen, Abendessen?*
Please may I have my key?	*Darf ich bitte meinen Schlüssel haben?*
Room number . . .	*Zimmer Nummer . . .*
Have you seen the others from my group (the party leader)?	*Haben Sie die anderen von meiner Gruppe (den Reiseleiter) gesehen?*
My friend (girl friend) is coming later	*Mein Freund (meine Freundin) kommt später*
Please may I have a packed lunch?	*Kann ich bitte ein Lunchpaket haben?*
Now, for tomorrow, early tomorrow morning	*Jetzt, für morgen, morgen früh*
I should like to take a bath/shower	*Ich möchte ein Bad, eine Dusche, nehmen*

At the ski shop Im Skigeschäft

The boots, skis, sticks	*Die Stiefel, Skier, Stöcke*
Too big, small, tight, loose	*Zu gross, klein, eng, locker*
Very expensive	*Sehr teuer*
Please can you adjust my binding?	*Können Sie bitte meine Bindung richten?*
Do you have another pair of boots?	*Haben Sie ein anderes Paar Stiefel?*
They hurt, they rub, they press	*Sie tun mir weh, sie reiben, sie drücken*
I am a beginner, intermediate	*Ich bin Anfänger, mittelmässig*
Advanced, a good skier	*fortgeschritten, ein guter Skifahrer*
I have come for the first (second, third, fourth) time	*Ich komme zum ersten (zweiten, dritten, vierten) Mal*
The ski hat, the gloves	*Die Mütze, die Handschuhe*
Sunglasses, goggles	*Sonnenbrille, Schneebrille*

At the souvenir shop Im Souvenirgeschäft

May I have a postcard please?	*Kann ich bitte eine Postkarte haben?*

Turn your shoulders; turn round	*Die Schulter drehen; umdrehen*
The ski run	*Die Abfahrt*
The ski lift, drag lift, chair lift	*Der Skilift, Schlepplift, Sessellift*
The cable car (or mountain railway)	*Die Bergbahn*
Top station, bottom station	*Bergstation, Talstation*
We meet at nine o'clock, quarter past nine, half past nine, a quarter to ten	*Wir treffen uns um neun Uhr, viertel nach neun, halb zehn, viertel vor zehn*
The meeting place for tomorrow is	*Der Treffpunkt für morgen ist*
I have lost my group (ski teacher)	*Ich habe meine Gruppe (Skilehrer) verloren*
I am hungry, thirsty, frightened	*Ich habe Hunger, Durst, Angst*
I am tired	*Ich bin müde*
I am cold, warm	*Mir ist kalt, warm*
I must go to the ski school at ten o'clock	*Ich muss um zehn Uhr zur Skischule gehen*
Tomorrow there is a race	*Morgen gibt es ein Wettrennen*
The prizegiving	*Die Preisverteilung*
To win a medal	*Ein Abzeichen gewinnen*
Bronze, silver, gold	*Bronze, Silber, Gold*

How much is a stamp for a letter (postcard) to England? — *Wie viel kostet eine Marke für einen Brief (eine Postkarte) nach England?*

Do you have English books, newspapers? — *Haben Sie englische Bücher, Zeitungen?*

Map, guide book — *Landkarte, Reiseführer*

Ashtray, doll, key ring — *Aschenbecher, Puppe, Schlüsselanhänger*

Wallet (or purse), pendant, mug, jug, glass — *Geldtasche, Anhänger, Becher, Krug, Glas*

Do you have a smaller, cheaper one? — *Haben Sie ein Kleineres, Billigeres?*

At the first aid station, at the doctor's — In der Erste Hilfe-Station, beim Arzt

My foot (leg, arm, head, shoulder) hurts	*Mein Fuss (Bein, Arm, Kopf, Schulter) tut weh*
My name is, I am called . . .	*Mein Name ist, ich heisse . . .*
My school is (is called) . . .	*Meine Schule ist (heisst) . . .*
My home address is . . .	*Meine Heimatadresse ist . . .*
How old are you?	*Wie alt sind Sie? (Wie alt bist Du?)*
I am fourteen, sixteen	*Ich bin vierzehn, sechzehn Jahre alt*
A sticking plaster, bandage, plaster cast	*Ein Pflaster, eine Bandage, ein Gips*
The insurance	*Die Versicherung*
You must not ski for two days	*Sie dürfen für zwei Tage nicht skifahren*

On the slopes — In der Skischule

Take your sticks like this	*Nehmen Sie die Stöcke so*
Copy me, do it like this	*Machen Sie mir nach, machen Sie es so*
Bend your knees, ankles, elbows	*Knie, Sprungelenke, Ellbogen beugen*
Upper body upright, stay upright	*Oberkörper aufrecht, aufrecht bleiben*
Don't sit down!	*Nicht sitzen!*
Come one by one, one behind the other	*Einzeln, hintereinander kommen*
More quickly, more slowly	*Schneller, langsamer*
Jump, lift one ski	*Springen, einen Ski heben*
Keep your ski tips on the ground	*Die Skispitzen am Boden lassen*
Lean out (downhill)	*Talwärts beugen*
Straight run, snowplough, traverse	*Schuss, Schneepflug, Schrägfahrt*
Basic turn, parallel turn	*Grundschwung, Parallelschwung*
Sideslip, uphill turn	*Seitrutschen, Schwung zum Hang*
That's good, bad, terrible	*Das ist gut, schlecht, furchtbar*
Please show us (me) once more	*Bitte zeigen Sie uns (mir) noch einmal*
I have hurt myself	*Ich habe mir weh getan*
Uphill side, downhill side, uphill ski, downhill ski	*Bergseite, Talseite, Bergski, Talski*
The inside edge, outside edge	*Die Innenkante, Aussenkante*
Put your weight on the downhill ski	*Den Talski belasten*

Italian for skiers

Do you understand English/Italian?	*Capisce l'inglese/l'italiano?*
Yes, no, a little	*Si, no, un poco*
Please speak slowly	*Per favore parli lentamente*
Good morning, good day, good evening	*Buon giorno, buona sera*
Good night	*Buona notte*
Goodbye	*Addio, arrivederci*
Do you like dancing? Do you like skiing?	*Le piace ballare? Le piace sciare?*
I must be in the hotel by ten o'clock	*Devo essere in albergo per le dieci*
Thank you	*Grazie*
Excuse me	*Mi scusi*
Where is the toilet (the exit) please?	*Per favore dov'è la toilette? (l'uscita)*
One to ten	*Uno, due, tre, quattro, cinque, sei, sette, otto, nove, dieci*
Eleven to twenty	*Undici, dodici, tredici, quattordici, quindici, sedici, diciasette, diciotto, dicianove, venti*
Twenty-one to twenty-nine	*Ventuno, ventidue, ventitre, ventiquattro, venticinque, ventisei, ventisette, ventotto, ventinove*
Thirty to ninety	*Trenta, quaranta, cinquanta, sessanta, settanta, ottanta, novanta*
One hundred, two hundred	*Cento, duecento*
One thousand	*Mille*

At the cafe, restaurant Al caffè, ristorante

May I have a . . . please?	*Per favore, posso avere . . . ?*
What time you you open, close?	*A che ora apre/chiude?*
How much is . . . ?	*Quanto costa . . . ?*
Hot chocolate, coffee, tea, milk	*Cioccolato caldo, caffè, tè, latte*
Orange squash, natural lemon, a soft drink	*Aranciata, limonata, bibita analcoolica*
Fruit juice, grapefruit	*Succo di frutta, pompelmo*
Cake, chocolate cake, apple strudel	*Dolce, dolce di cioccolato, strudel di mele*

Open sandwich with cheese, cold meat	*Sandwich al formaggio, con carne fredda*
Frankfurters with bread, chips	*Panino con wurstel, patate fritte*
Goulasch, spaghetti, lasagne, vegetable soup, pancake, pizza	*Spezzatino, spaghetti, lasagne, minestrone, crepes, pizza*
Fried veal in breadcrumbs, with salad	*Cotoletta alla milanese con insalata*

At the hotel   All'albergo

What time is breakfast, lunch supper?	*A che ora è la prima colazione, il pranzo, la cena?*
Please may I have my key?	*Per favore posso avere la mia chiave?*
Please give me key number . . .	*Per favore mi da la chiave numero . . .*
Room number . . .	*Camera numero . . .*
Have you seen the others from my group (the party leader)?	*Ha visto gli altri membri del mio gruppo (il capo gruppo)?*
My friend (girl friend) is coming later	*Il mio amico (la mia amica) arriverà più tardi*
Please may I have a packed lunch?	*Per favore posso avere un cestino da viaggio?*
Now, for tomorrow, early tomorrow morning	*Ora, per domani, domani mattina presto*
I should like to take a bath/shower	*Vorrei prendere un bagno/doccia*

At the ski shop   Al negozio di sci

The boots, skis, sticks	*Gli scarponi, gli sci, i bastoncini*
Too big, small, tight, loose	*Troppo grande, piccolo, stretto, largo*
Very expensive	*Molto caro*
Please can you adjust my binding?	*Per favore può aggiustare i miei attachi?*
Do you have another pair of boots?	*Ha un altro paio di scarponi?*
They hurt, they rub, they press	*Fanno male, graffiano, premono*
I am a beginner, intermediate advanced, a good skier	*Io sono un principiante, uno sciatore medio, un esperto, un buon sciatore*
I have come for the first (second, third, fourth) time	*Sono venuto per la prima (seconda, terza, quarta) volta*
The ski hat, the gloves	*Il cappello da sci, i guanti*
Sunglasses, goggles	*Occhiali da sole, occhiali da sci*

Put your weight on the downhill ski	*Poggiate sullo sci a valle*
Turn your shoulders, turn round	*Girate le spalle, giratevi*
The ski run	*La discesa, la pista*
The ski lift, drag lift, chair lift	*Lo ski lift, seggiovia*
The cable car (or mountain railway)	*La funivia*
Top station, bottom station	*Stazione a monte, stazione a valle*
We meet at nine o'clock, half past nine, quarter past nine, a quarter to ten	*Ci vediamo alle nove, alle nove e mezzo, alle nove e un quarto, alle dieci meno un quarto*
The meeting place for tomorrow is . . .	*Il luogo di incontro per domani è . . .*
I have lost my group (ski teacher)	*Ho perduto il mio gruppo (maestro di sci)*
I am hungry, thirsty, frightened	*Ho fame, ho sete, ho paura*
I am tired	*Sono stanco*
I am cold, warm	*Ho freddo, caldo*
I must go to the ski school at ten o'clock	*Devo andare alla scuola di sci alle dieci*
Tomorrow there is a race	*Domani ci sarà una gara*
The prizegiving	*La distribuzione dei premi*
To win a medal	*Vincere una medaglia*
Bronze, silver, gold	*Bronzo, argento, oro*

At the souvenir shop — Al negozio di ricordi

May I have a postcard please?	*Mi da una cartolina, per favore?*
How much is a stamp for a letter (postcard) to England?	*Quanto costa un francobollo per una lettera (una cartolina) per l'Inghilterra*
Do you have English books, newspapers?	*Ha libri inglesi, giornali?*
Map, guide book	*Piantina, guida*
Ashtray, doll, key ring	*Portacenere, bambola, portachiavi*
Wallet (or purse), pendant, mug, jug, glass	*Portafoglia (porta monete), pendant, vaso, bricca, bicchiere*
Do you have a smaller, cheaper one?	*Ne ha uno più piccolo, uno meno caro?*

At the first aid station, at the doctor's — Al pronto soccorso, al medico

My foot (leg, arm, head, shoulder) hurts	*Il mio piede (la mia gamba, testa, spalla) mi fa male*
My name is, I am called . . .	*Il mio nome è, io mi chiamo . . .*
My school is (is called) . . .	*La mia scuola è (si chiama) . . .*
My home address is . . .	*Il mio indirizzo di casa è . . .*
How old are you?	*Che età hai?*
I am fourteen, sixteen	*Ho quattordici anni, sedici anni*
A sticking plaster, bandage, plaster cast	*Un cerotto, benda, gesso*
The insurance	*L'assicurazione*
You must not ski for two days	*Non devi sciare per due giorni*

On the slopes — Sulli pisti

Take your sticks like this	*Prendi i bastoncini così*
Copy me, do it like this	*Imitate me, fate così*
Bend your knees, ankles, elbows	*Piegate i ginocchi, le caviglie, i gomiti*
Upper body upright, stay upright	*Parte superiore del corpo eretta, state eretti*
Don't sit down!	*Non vi sedete!*
Come one by one, one behind the other	*Venite uno per volta, uno dietro l'altro*
More quickly, more slowly	*Più in fretta, più lentamente*
Jump, lift one ski	*Saltate, sollevate uno sci*
Keep your ski tips on the ground	*Tenete la punta degli sci per terra*
Touch your boots	*Toccate gli scarponi*
Lean out (downhill)	*Sporgere verso valle*
Straight run, snowplough, traverse	*Andare diritto, spazza neve, diagonale*
Basic turn, parallel turn	*Girata elementare, curva a sci parallele*
Sideslip, uphill turn	*Derapata, girata a monte*
That's good, bad, terrible	*Così va bene, non va bene, terribile*
Please show us (me) once more	*Per favore mi mostri ancora una volta*
I have hurt myself	*Mi sono fatto male*
Uphill side, downhill side, uphill ski, downhill ski	*A monte, a valle, sci a monte, sci a valle*
The inside edge, outside edge	*Lamina interna, lamina esterna*

Glossary

Angulation
A forward bending at the hips, as the upper body tends to follow its momentum when the legs are turned to steer the skis.

Basic swing
Rhythmically linked turns with ploughed and skidded phases, which are used to learn the essential elements of parallel skiing.

Cable car
In German: *Luftseilbahn*; in French: *Télépherique*; in Italian: *Funivia*. Uphill transport consisting of a cabin suspended from an overhead cable.

Camber
The arch that is built into the ski enabling the skier's weight to be distributed along the entire running surface of the ski.

Canting
Altering the angle of the boot on the ski, in order to compensate for way individuals stand on skis.

Chair lift
In German: *Sesselbahn*; in French: *Télésiège*; in Italian: *Seggiovia*. Uphill transport consisting of double or single seater chairs suspended from an overhead cable. Skis can be worn or carried.

Christiania (Christie)
A turn made with skis parallel. Named after the district now called Oslo in Norway.

Clock or star turn
A method of changing direction on the flat. Its name derives from the pattern left in the snow after a complete turn.

Compression turns
In German: *Wellen*; in French: *Avalement*; in Italian: *Assorbimento*. A turning technique in which the legs are turned whilst bending and extending to keep a constant pressure between the soles of the skis and the snow.

Drag lift
An overhead cable system with attachments by which skiers are pulled up a slope. Variations are the poma or button lift, and the T-bar designed for two persons to travel side by side.

Edging
The lateral tilting of the skis towards the slope. Used to control the sideways movement of the skis.

Egg position
A crouched position used in racing to minimise wind resistance.

Fall line
The imaginary line which follows the steepest gradient of a slope.

FIS
Federation Internationale de Ski, the international governing body of skiing.

Föhn
A warm wind which blows onto the Alps from the south.

Herringbone
A climbing step with skis in a V-shape open at the tips. The name derives from the pattern left in the snow.

Inside ski
The ski on the inside of the turning arc.

Kick turn
Changing direction through 180° in a standing position across a slope.

Kilometro Lanciato
The Flying Kilometre. The competition to attack the world speed record on the upper slopes of Cervinia, Italy.

Lapse rate
The rate at which the temperature drops as you gain altitude.

Linked turns
Continuous turning down a slope where one turn leads straight into the next.

Lower ski
The ski on the downhill side of the slope.

Moguls
Large rounded bumps on the ski slope formed sometimes by the terrain under the snow but usually by the action of many skiers turning repeatedly in the same place.

Nursery slopes
Gentle gradients where beginners first learn to ski.

Outside ski
The ski on the outside of the turning arc.

Parallel skiing
Edges are changed simultaneously, whilst turning and skis are parallel throughout the descent.

Piste
Marked and prepared ski runs.

Release bindings
The mechanisms which secure the boot to the skis. They are designed to release the boots at a pre-determined pressure. The adjustments which determine the point of release must be made in relation to the skill, weight, strength and size of the skier.

Retaining strap
Strap attached to binding and skier to stop the ski running away after it has been released (see also Ski brake).

Schuss
Straight running down the fall line with skis parallel.

Short swings
Used on steeper terrain; short quick turns with pronounced edge set helping to control downhill speed.

Side slip
A sideways movement of the skis due to release of edges and the pull of gravity.

Side stepping
A climbing step with skis on their uphill edges horizontally across the fall line.

Ski patrol
The organisation responsible for policing the ski area. They are concerned with safety on the pistes, ambulancing and directing ski traffic.

Ski brake
A sprung mechanical device which operates to prevent the ski from running down the hill when the boot is released from the binding.

Slalom
Controlled downhill skiing between gates. These are pairs of red and blue flags. Giant slalom is a faster version of special slalom.

Traverse
Movement across a slope holding a line.

Unweighting
Moving the body in relation to the skis to bring about a reduction of weight between skis and snow. Unweighting facilitates edge change and turning the skis.

Wedeln
Continuous rhythmical linked turns close to the fall line with very little edge set.

Index

Page references in italics refer to photographs or illustrations.

Accident procedure 29
Amstutz, Walter 84, *84*, 86
Angulation 53, 55, 57, *57*, 59, *59*
Anorak 22
Après ski 16, 23
Artificial ski slopes 74, *74*, 75, *75*
Assorbimento 61, *61*
Avalanche 28, *29*
Avalement 61, *61*

Bartelski, Konrad 14, *14*
Basic swing 55, *55, 61, 61*
Beck, Lesley 15
Bell, Martin 14, 15, *15*
Biathlon 9, 10, *10*, 77
Bindings 25, *25, 32, 32*, 35, *35*, 84, *84*, 85, *85*, 86, 87
Blanc, Robert 85, *85*
Blizzards 26, 28
Boots 24, 25, *25, 32, 32*, 33, *33*, 84, *84*, 85, 86, 87
Bracken, Bill 81, *81*
Breyton, Catherine 13

Christiania 80, *81*, 83
Clock turn 38, *38*
Clothing 22, *22*, 23, *23*
Compression turns 60, *60, 61, 61*
Cross country skiing 10, *10*, 76, *76*, 77

Direct method 58, *58*
Downhill 17, 73, *73*

Egg position 73, *73*
Engadine Marathon 10
Erskine, Malcolm 71

FIS 6, 9
Fall line 40
Falling over 30, 44, *44*, 45, *45*
Fan method 59, *59*
Fellows, Nick 15, *15*
Fitness 18-21, *18-21*
Fjelstad, Torill 7
Four Hills Tournament 11
Freestyle 12, *12*

Galicia, Davina 14
Garrison, Jim *12*
Giant Slalom 6, 7, 72
Greene, Nancy 6

Hathorn, Gina 14, *85*
Herringbone 41, *41*
High Route 78, 79, *79*
Hot dog skiing 12, *12*
Hoting ski 80, *80*, 85

Ice 27, 66, 68, 69, *69*

Kandahar Cup 5, 81
Killy, Jean Claude 6, *83*
Klammer, Franz 8, *9*
Kogler, Armin 10, 11

Lapse rate 26, 67
Lewis, Sarah 15, *15*
Lift passes 16
Lunn, Sir Arnold 81, 83

McKinney, Steve 13, *13*
Macintosh, Christopher 82, *82*

Maher, Phil 5, 6, *54*
Meals 16, 19
Moguls 61, 62, *62*, 63, *63*, 66, *66*
Moser-Proell, Anne Marie 5, 6, 7, *7*
Muira, Yuichiro 78
Muller, Peter 6

Olympic Games *4*, 5, 8, *8*, 9, *9*, 10, *10*, 11, *11*, 77

Palmer-Tomkinson, Jeremy 14
Parallel turns 52, *52*, 53, *53*, 54, *54*, 56, *56*, 57, *57*, 58, *58*, 59, *59*, 61, *61*
Pelen, Perrine *72*
Pinching, Evie 81, *81*
Piste maps 17, *17*
Plough swing 53, *53*
Podborski, Steve 6
Powder snow 27, 29, 68, *68*, 69
Pre-jump 73, *73*
Proell, Cornelia 7

Read, Ken 6
Rowan, Mark 13, *73*

Sailer, Toni 83
Salopette 22
Serrat, Fabienne *64*
Schnabl, Karl 11, *11*
Schnieder, Hannes 83
Schussing 43, *43*
Short swings 65, *65*
Side slipping 51, *51*
Side stepping 41, *41*
Skating turn 71, *71*
Ski brakes (retaining straps) 32, *32*, 36, *36*, 87
Ski Council 15, 75
Ski flying 11
Ski jumping 11, *11*
Ski lifts 16, 30, *30*, 31, *31*, 49
Ski resorts 16
Ski school 32, *36*, 37, 85, 86, 87, *87*
Ski tests 75
Ski touring 76, *76*, 77
Skis 25, *25, 32, 32*, 33, *33*, 34, *34*, 36, *36*, 37, *37*, 45, 49, 84, *84*, 85, 86, 87
Skiway Code 29
Slalom 6, 7, 70, 72, *81*
Slope hanging 42, *42*
Smetanina, Reiser 11
Smith, Nigel 15
Snow conditions 27, 66, *66*, 67, *67*
Snowplough 46, *46*, 47, *47*
Snowplough turn 48, *48*, 49, *49*
Spiess, Uli 6
Stenmark, Ingemar *4, 4*, 5, *5*, 6, *6*, 8, 9, 22
Step turn 39, *39*, 70, *70*
Sticks 25, 35, *35*, 55, *55*, 58, 62, 84, 85, 86, 87
Sunburn 24, 26

Telemark turn 81, *81*
Traversing *24*, 50, *51*

Unweighting 56, 64, 71, *71*

Walking on skis 38, *38*
Wassberg, Thomas 10
Weight training 21, *21*
Wellen 61, *61*
White out 26, *26*, 28
World Championships 5, 9, *9*
World Cup *4*, 5, 6, *6*, 7, *7*
World Speed Record 13, *13*

Zardski, Mathias 80
Zavjalov, Alexandre 10
Zhirov, Alexander 6, *7*

You and your group

Name..

School..

Resort...

Hotel..

Dates of tour..

Best moment of tour ....

....

....

....

....

....

....

....

....

....

....

....

Use the space on the opposite page to:
a) Collect the autographs of everyone in your group (including teachers)
b) Stick in a postcard or photograph of your resort and/or hotel.
c) Attach a photograph or colour a picture of the national flag.